T0330967

Routledge Revivals

The Economic Theory of Fiscal Policy

Originally published in 1971, this book uses the famous Tinbergen/Theil approach to the theory of economic policy, demonstrating the place of fiscal policy in a realistic policy context. The volume marries analytical developments in macroeconomics to the influence on the economy of the system of public finance. Attention is given to the problem co-ordinating fiscal policy with other policy instruments, notably monetary policy. A final chapter discusses the problems encountered in applying fiscal policy models to real situations.

The Economic Theory of Fiscal Policy

Alan T. Peacock and G.K. Shaw.

First published in 1971 by George Allen & Unwin Ltd

This edition first published in 2024 by Routledge
4 Park Square, Milton Park, Abingdon, Oxon, OX14 4RN
and by Routledge
605 Third Avenue, New York, NY 10158.

Routledge is an imprint of the Taylor & Francis Group, an informa business

ISBN 13: 978-1-032-82172-6 (hbk)
ISBN 13: 978-1-003-50331-6 (ebk)
ISBN 13: 978-1-032-82175-7 (pbk)
Book DOI 10.4324/9781003503316

THE ECONOMIC THEORY OF FISCAL POLICY

by
Alan Peacock
Professor of Economics, University of York
and
G. K. Shaw
Lecturer in Economics, University of York

London
GEORGE ALLEN AND UNWIN LTD

FIRST PUBLISHED IN 1971

© *George Allen and Unwin Ltd., 1971*

ISBN 0 04 330166 5 cloth
   0 04 330167 3 paper

PRINTED IN GREAT BRITAIN BY
ALDEN & MOWBRAY LTD
AT THE ALDEN PRESS, OXFORD

CONTENTS

PREFACE

This book seeks to answer the question what can economic analysis tell us about the effects of various fiscal measures on the value of those macroeconomic variables whose movements are taken as a guide to the performance of the economy, e.g. income, output, employment, growth, prices and the balance of payments. Its point of departure is the conventional macroeconomic model, embodying government taxation and expenditure, which still dominates even fairly advanced textbooks in economics and is the implicit model in much of the popular journalistic discussion of fiscal policy. The shortcomings of the conventional model have been clearly recognized in the growing economics literature associated with the theory of economic policy. Briefly put, these shortcomings are the association of the problem of maintaining stability with only one important economic variable, the level of money income, and the *simpliste* nature of the economic system which is embodied in the model.

A fair proportion of the professional literature on the theory of economic policy employs very sophisticated tools of analysis, and this accounts for the difficulty of translating it into terms more familiar to the economist specializing in public finance. In seeking to answer the general question referred to, we have used simpler mathematical techniques, while still conveying, so it is hoped, the important improvements in the formulation of the analysis of policy problems which the theory of economic policy has provided.

Fortunately, it is now common practice in reputable universities to insist that undergraduates specializing in economics must be able to understand mathematical models and to discern their relevance in the formulation of policy problems. It is a sign of the revolution in economics education that we can state with some confidence that a student who has grasped the elements of mathematical economics should have no difficulty in following this text. Therefore, we hope

9

that it will be a useful addition to the literature recommended for macroeconomics courses from the intermediate level upwards, and for public finance courses for undergraduates and graduate students in which the economics of fiscal policy plays a substantial role. At the same time, we believe that economists closely involved in research and policy-making in government and business may find it useful to consult a work which offers a conspectus of recent academic thinking on matters which are their day-to-day concern. This belief rests on more than faith in the need for a constant dialogue between theorist and practitioner, but upon our own occasional employment as consultants to governments and international organizations. Indeed, the choice of illustrations of the use of particular models have been influenced considerably by the investigations we have been asked to undertake for such bodies.

Some of the text of this volume re-works previous contributions by the authors to professional journals. Acknowledgement is made to these sources at the appropriate place, but in few instances have we left the original text unchanged. Various of our academic colleagues have been persuaded to comment on particular sections of the work. We would like to thank in particular Mr. Michael Jones-Lee for a barrage of suggestions and criticisms. For permission to use hitherto unpublished material we are especially indebted to Professor Robert W. Kilpatrick of Cornell University. We are most grateful to both the Department of Economics and the Institute of Social and Economic Research for typing assistance, and hope that Miss Mary Robinson and Mrs Susan Loft of these institutions respectively will acquire no long-standing aversion to the Greek alphabet in the course of their much appreciated labours. Finally, Alan Peacock would like to record his warm appreciation of the use of the facilities of the Fondazione Luigi Einaudi, Turin, Italy, where, as a visiting research professor, he was able to complete some necessary revisions to part of the manuscript.

A.P.
G.K.S.

PART ONE

THE MACROECONOMIC ANALYSIS OF FISCAL POLICY

Chapter I

THE SCOPE OF THE WORK

I. INTRODUCTION

The purpose of this work is to offer a review of the economics of fiscal policy which takes account of some major post-Keynesian developments in macroeconomic theory (1). While both the theory and the public finance measures which influence the economy will have been studied by those likely to read this volume, the authors have been struck by the paucity of attempts to bring them both together. On the one hand, macroeconomic models, which have undergone rapid transformation in the hands of such writers as Harrod, Hicks, Samuelson, Solow, Kaldor, Kalecki and Domar, rarely specify the transactions of the system of public finance in sufficient detail in order to understand their influence on the economy. On the other hand, writers of public finance text-books have employed models of the economy in studying, for example, the possibility of achieving economic stability by budgetary means, which can only be described as *simpliste*. There are notable exceptions to this criticism (2), but at the time of writing the attempts at marrying the recent analytical developments in macroeconomics and the influence of the system of public finance on the economy are largely buried in the covers of professional academic journals.

In order to explain how the attempt is made to bridge the gap between the innovations in economic analytics and their application to the study of fiscal policy, it is necessary to say something about some recent developments in economic theory. The rest of this

(1) For a comprehensive review of the theory, see R. G. D. Allen, *Macro-Economic Theory*, London, 1968.
(2) Such as Bent Hansen, *The Economic Theory of Fiscal Policy*, 1958; R. A. Musgrave, *The Theory of Public Finance*, 1959; L. Johansen, *Public Economics*, 1965; and Carl Shoup, *Public Finance*, 1969.

introductory chapter discusses some of these developments and in so doing offers a rationale for the scope and content of this work.

II. THE KEYNESIAN ANALYSIS OF FISCAL POLICY

A fairly standard treatment of the economic theory of fiscal policy in text-books on public finance may be caricatured in the following way. A 'target' national income (= expenditure) is chosen as being consistent with the objective of 'full employment' (of labour). This target is a unique value of a dependent variable, national income, which is influenced by several exogeneously determined variables some of which are assumed under government control. The government, through the system of public finance, is made to influence the size of the national expenditure, usually in two ways. Government expenditure on goods and services is itself a component of national expenditure. Variations in government revenue, usually represented only by a proportional tax on personal income, can affect the level of consumer expenditure on goods and services, which is usually the major component (in size) of national expenditure. All that the government need do in order to stabilize the economy at the 'target' level of income (and therefore employment) is to alter the proportional income tax rate or the size of government expenditure, the amount of the alteration depending on the value of the Keynesian multiplier. A breath of realism can be introduced into the analysis by placing certain constraints on government action, such as the requirement that politicians do not like unbalanced budgets. It can then be shown that achieving the desired target is still possible, but requires larger changes in government expenditure and income, because of the (assumed) smaller multiplier effect of a balanced budget. Or, it may be assumed that both tax rates and expenditure rates are difficult to change in the short run, and simple economic analysis is used to show that all is not lost, because some taxes and transfer payments (e.g. unemployment benefits) are automatic stabilizers.

This caricature is only a means of directing attention to the salient features of common text-book presentation, and allowance must be made for the fact that even within the narrow scope offered by the simple model of income determination, many variations in exposition and in content are possible. Also, it may be argued, as, indeed we accept in Chapter II, that the simple Keynesian theory of income determination is a reasonable point of departure for the study of fiscal policy designed to achieve economic stability. However, it is little more than this.

If we wish to develop a model which may offer a framework for policy-making, we must go much further, as an examination of the omissions from the simple analysis will indicate.

III. EXTENDING AND MODIFYING THE SIMPLE KEYNESIAN MODEL

Let it be assumed for the moment that the main interest of the model lies in examining the effects of the budget on the level of national income. The model may be said to be incomplete in the sense that there are other influences on the level of national income which either influence that level directly or through the independent variables, consumption, investment, already identified. The most obvious example is the neglect in the basic Keynesian equation of income determination of the influence of the monetary system. As Chapter II indicates, even simple assumptions, such as the exogenous determination of the money supply, the determination of the rate of interest by money supply and the level of national income, and the dependence of the level of investment on the rate of interest, offer substantial modifications to the simplified analysis. It is to be noted that these modifications are carried out within the 'standard' Keynesian framework, which assumes that changes in the supply of money affect the level of income only via changes in the rate of interest and hence in the level of investment. One does not need to invoke neo-classical monetary theory which would have us regard the level of *consumption* as a function of changes in the quantity of money (3).

One important corollary of the introduction of the monetary system is that, in estimating the effects of fiscal policy on the level of income, we have to specify clearly the assumptions being made about monetary policy. It must also be noted in passing that budget changes

---

(3) For a clear and relatively simple exposition of classical macroeconomics, see Gardner Ackley, *Macroeconomic Theory*, 1961. For a more specific analysis of monetary theory and consumption see Don Patinkin, *Money, Interest and Prices*, 2nd edition, Harper International edition, 1966.

themselves, in so far as these result in government surpluses and deficits, may affect the supply of money depending on whether surpluses draw cash from and deficits push cash into the economic system.

The introduction of the monetary system does not extend the number of terms in the basic income equation $Y = C+I+G$, but makes it unnecessary for I to be treated as an autonomous variable in order to solve for Y, i.e. by making I dependent on the rate of interest, and the rate of interest dependent on the supply of money as well as the level of income. A more obvious indication of the deficiencies of the simple Keynesian fiscal policy model is to be found in the assumption of a closed economy. Chapter III of this volume examines what happens when this assumption is removed and the income equation is extended to include the balance of payments. Controlling the level of Y by taxes and government expenditure becomes, therefore, a complex matter, when the level of income itself depends on transactions with other countries. It becomes even more complex when fiscal policy has to take account not only of the degree of 'openness' of the economy but also of the effects of monetary policy on the balance of payments, in judging the correct adjustments to be made in achieving the 'target' level of income.

It was early realized in the development of modern macroeconomic theory that the relation between changes in investment and consumption and changes in income were not independent of the degree of aggregation of economic transactions. This point has often been illustrated by dividing consumers into 'workers' and 'capitalists', the former having a marginal propensity to consume of unity and the latter a marginal propensity to consume of less than unity. A redistribution of income brought about by fiscal means, e.g. by the differential impact of taxes and/or transfer payments, between workers and capitalists would therefore alter the aggregated marginal propensity to consume and, consequently, the level of national income. If it were desired to raise the level of national income, this could be done by making the distribution of disposable income (factor income + transfers − taxes) more equal and vice versa if policy demanded a lowering of the level of national income. Many variations can be developed on the theme of disaggregation, and the authors of this volume have chosen to concentrate on the less familiar but equally interesting cases (from the policy point of view) of the disaggregation of government expenditure by type of purchase, and disaggregation of budget transactions by layer of government (see Chapter IV). The first example enables us to introduce the reader to the integration of input–output analysis with the Keynesian-type macroeconomic system including a public sector. The second attempts to illustrate how fiscal policy can be introduced into the type of disaggregated model increasingly employed in regional economics. Once again, the paradox of Keynesian-type models is displayed: their receptivity to adaptation and extension, and their basic simplicity.

IV. THE 'TARGET VARIABLE' AMBIGUITY

So far, we have shown how the Keynesian-type model needs modification in order to take account of the structure of actual economic systems, but throughout the process of modification, it has invariably been assumed that the basic purpose of the analysis is to determine the effects of fiscal policy on the level of national income, the target variable.

The concentration of interest on this target variable arose from the association of fluctuations in employment of labour with fluctuations in income. Given the widespread acceptance of the need for full employment of labour, it is a simple step to assume that the task of fiscal policy is to stabilize national income at a level compatible with this objective. The function $N = N(Y)$, where N is the number of employed persons, and Y, money national income, clearly telescopes a chain of reasoning which begins at one end with the proposition that $N = N(Q, w)$, where Q is national output and w 'the' wage rate, and $Q = Q(Y)$, i.e. output is a function of the level of aggregate demand or money national income.

As is well known, Keynes was one of the first to recognize that increases in aggregate demand in conditions where all resources are fully employed, will result in the short run in an increase in the general price level and not in an increase in employment. The general acceptance of avoidance of inflation leads to the first important dichotomy in the objective function denoting economic stability into 'full employment of labour' and 'price stability'. In order to cope with the problem of associating changes in employment with changes

B

in output, Keynesian models have been squared with the traditional marginal productivity theory of factor inputs by assuming: (a) that the marginal = average productivity of labour; (b) that up to the full employment level, 'the' wage rate is constant; and (c) that in the short run an increase in investment only affects the level of demand and not the level of output. These assumptions make it possible to assume that the aggregate supply curve is horizontal up to the full employment level, and that employment is a linear function of aggregate supply (output). Beyond the full employment point, the aggregate supply function has an elasticity of zero and any increase in aggregate demand results in a proportional increase in the general price level (4).

The result of these subterfuges in assumption-making appears to have been designed to hold to the proposition that fiscal policy still need only keep national income at that unique level at which full employment is achieved and inflation is just about to begin. However, we cannot be content to accept this 'let-out', even although, as Chapter V indicates, the adoption of more realistic assumptions leads to analytical complications. We must take account of recent empirical research which denies that full employment, as a political objective, is compatible with stable prices. We must also take into account the fact that the tax system impinges on the economy not solely in the form of taxes on incomes but also in the form of taxes on goods and services. These latter—consumption taxes are an obvious example—require us to look more closely at the reactions of producers to tax changes, and how these are reflected in their pricing decisions and in their demand for labour.

V. THE SHORT PERIOD AND THE LONG PERIOD

So far we have examined quite a number of ways in which the simple Keynesian model must be modified in order to define the task of fiscal policy, given the single objective of maintaining full employment without inflation. As yet, the model in all its variants deals only with the short run, during which period of time the labour force is constant in size, and changes in the capital stock reflected in altera-

---

(4) See, for example, Martin Bronfenbrenner and Frank D. Holzman, 'A Survey of Inflation Theory', *Surveys of Economic Theory*, Vol. I, 1965.

tions in *I* affect only the level of money national income and not the level of (potential) national output. In the longer run, it is manifest that neither of these assumptions will hold.

It is not necessary to describe in any detail how the Keynesian short-period model has been transformed into the Harrod–Domar type growth model, for the process is familiar even to first-year economics students (5). Preserving economic stability, in the sense of maintaining full employment without inflation, now requires the adjustment of aggregate demand to a growth *path* of output and employment and not to a unique level of national income. The interesting problem encountered in using fiscal weapons for this purpose is that one has to bear in mind that tax and expenditure changes may not only affect the level of aggregate demand, but also the growth path itself. An obvious example is an increase in government expenditure on education which, *ceteris paribus*, increases aggregate demand, but at the same time, adds to the stock of capital and is therefore likely to increase potential output through the improvement in skills.

Chapter VI follows standard practice in demonstrating how budgetary transactions can be introduced into the simple Harrod–Domar growth model, but the model itself does not include an explicit functional relationship between output and employment but only between output and the growth in the capital stock. One way round this difficulty is to assume that labour and capital are employed in fixed proportions. This means that the task of the fiscal system becomes the rather complicated one of marrying the growth in capital stock to the growth in the labour force and ensuring that aggregate demand is just sufficient to absorb the resultant output.

However, it is now widely accepted in economics that the assumption of fixed proportions is an extreme one and that it is more reasonable to assume that elasticity of substitution between capital and labour is positive. Recent discussion of growth theory has been largely dominated by the use of models which postulate constant returns to scale and an elasticity of substitution between capital and labour of unity, as in the simple version of the Cobb–Douglas

---

(5) Cf. a well-known text such as D. M. McDougall and T. E. Dernberg, *Macroeconomics*, Student International edition, 1963, Chapter 16.

Function (6). Such models demonstrate that the economy automatically adjusts to the long-run growth in the labour force, thus, apparently, making fiscal adjustments designed to achieve full employment unnecessary. Chapter VI shows that this extreme conclusion assumes that the community is indifferent to the speed of adjustment to the equilibrium growth level which produces full employment and also that technical progress is ignored. We are able to show that fiscal policy still has a role to play, when these factors are brought into reckoning.

One further important point about the study of the long period is that it concentrates attention on other policy objectives of interest to the community, such as provision of a 'satisfactory' rate of growth in income and/or consumption per head, alongside a 'satisfactory' employment level. We shall show later that the move away from the traditional Keynesian 'one-target' model to a 'multi-target' one offers the opportunity of integrating the analysis of fiscal policy with what is now termed the theory of economic policy. All that need be said here is that we shall show that the Keynesian analysis of fiscal policy emerges as a special case within the theory of economic policy in which there is only *one* objective and *one* policy instrument, whereas in any policy situation we encounter several objectives and several policy instruments. (Cf. Section VII below.)

VI. TIME AND ECONOMIC STABILITY

The theory of income determination is usually carried out in the form of an exercise in 'comparative statics'. An equilibrium level of national income is postulated, a change takes place in one of the independent variables, and 'hey presto' a new level of national income is determined. It is clear that any such adjustment from one level of income to another must take time, so the analysis either is being totally unrealistic by assuming instantaneous adjustment, or incomplete in not specifying the time path. It is also implicit that, in the process of adjustment, no further disturbances take place after the intial change in one of the independent variables, or simultaneous initial change in more than one.

---

(6) For an excellent exposition of neo-classical growth theory, see F. H. Hahn and R. C. O. Matthews, 'The Theory of Economic Growth: A Survey', *Surveys of Economic Theory*, Vol. II, 1965.

Time more clearly enters the picture in growth models, for changes in the size of working population and capital stock and resultant changes in the flow of output postulate a time continuum. Nevertheless, the use of any policy instrument, such as a change in tax rates, is completely independent of the time period of adjustment. For example, if the growth rate requires to be raised, say by raising the annual rate of investment, a change in one of the fiscal parameters to achieve this end is immediately reflected in a change in the growth rate.

One of the earliest and most fruitful modifications of the Keynesian comparative static model was designed to explain the observed phenomenon of cyclical movements through time in income and employment. The famous Samuelson combination of the multiplier and the accelerator, which traced out such fluctuations, given that the consumption coefficient and accelerator assumed values within a certain range, was able to arrive at this result by the plausible assumption of lagged adjustment. Thus, consumption was made a lagged function of income and investment a lagged function of the rate of change in consumption (or in later formulations, income). It is rather surprising that the reformulation of the income equation as a second-order difference equation did not embrace fiscal variables at a much earlier stage than occurred. The Samuelson equation appeared in 1939, the equation plus fiscal variables not until 1961. What we are able to show (Chapter VII), building on recent analysis, is that both discretionary and automatic changes in fiscal policy can in some circumstances be de-stabilizing, as a consequence of the lagged responses of fiscal changes, to changes in the level of national income. Similarly, we can show that automatic changes in tax yields without changes in tax rates can result in aggregate demand falling below what is required to maintain stable growth, as compared with the common conclusion in the static Keynesian model that the built-in stability resulting from the tax system can never fully compensate for any autonomous shift in one of the independent variables which results in a rise (fall) in income.

VII. THE 'TRADE-OFF' PROBLEM

As already mentioned, the simple type of analysis of fiscal policy asks the questions: 'What determines the level of national income?' and

'How can the level of national income be influenced by fiscal means in order to achieve economic stability?' We have, so far, concentrated largely on the procedures which must be followed in developing satisfactory models which seek to answer the first of these questions. It is now time to consider in more detail the content of the second.

Perhaps the best way of considering the second question is to list the macroeconomic variables which are associated with economic stability. Those singled out for special consideration are the level of employment, the general level of prices and exports and imports (the balance of payments). Thus it is commonly accepted that values of these variables must be attained which ensure full employment of labour, a stable (or gently rising) price level and 'equilibrium' in the balance of payments, i.e. no deficits in the balance of payments with a fixed exchange rate. The simultaneous achievement of all these elements of economic stability, as is plain from recent economic history, is difficult enough to attain, but stability does not exhaust the list of policy objectives whose fulfilment is supposed to be influenced by the fiscal system. In Section V above, we mentioned recent interest in the growth performance of the economy, and one might add in a 'satisfactory' distribution of income and even wealth. It would be pure chance, therefore, if some specific value of Y would represent a bliss point at which all these objectives would be simultaneously reached.

We also saw earlier (Section III) that the effectiveness of fiscal policy depends on what assumptions are made about the monetary system and how monetary policy is assumed to operate. In short, we have to know something about the degree of *co-ordination* in the use of policy instruments. Likewise, the effectiveness of any given fiscal policy depends upon the *choice of objectives*, and the relative weight assigned to each one. In the language of the economic pundits, we have to specify the community's 'social welfare (or objective) function'.

It is for this reason that we have turned in the latter part of this volume to consider the place of fiscal policy within the framework of the theory of economic policy, associated particularly with the Dutch economists, Tinbergen and Theil (7). Briefly put, what the theory of

(7) See Jan Tinbergen, 'On the Theory of Economic Policy', *Contributions to Economic Analysis*, 2nd edition, Vol. I, Amsterdam, 1952, and Henri Theil,

economic policy does is to explore the analogy between the maximization of utility by an individual economic unit (consumer, producer) subject to constraints and by the government as the body responsible for meeting the community's desired objectives. Policy targets are specified, such as those listed in the last paragraph, and are embodied in a community objective function. These are the dependent variables in the relevant economic model. Policy instruments are then specified, and these are reflected in the independent variables in the economic model. The essential problem which the theory of economic policy tries to solve is that of devising a feasible combination of targets and instruments, subject to the constraints presented by the structure of the economy. The structure of the economy is, of course, represented by the system of equations which embody the economic model. (For further discussion, see Chapters VIII and IX.) Within this framework, we can examine how far fiscal policy is the appropriate instrument among the set of instruments available to the government to achieve any particular target or set of targets.

It may be useful to offer a diagrammatic representation of the methodology of the theory of economic policy, but with special reference to the role of fiscal policy (see schema overleaf). In this schema, social welfare is a function of two objectives, the 'desired' rate of growth, Y^r, defined as the rate of increase in real output, Y, and of economic stability, i.e. *ex ante* saving, S_x, and investment, I_x, have to be equal at the full employment of resources level. These two policy objectives may be influenced via the effect on the economic system as described in the model by fiscal policy instruments. The hatched lines merely denote that, in other contexts, other objectives and other policy instruments may be relevant.

One point worth noting in passing is that we have assumed that the social welfare function is maximized by achieving the *target* rate of growth and the equality of savings and investment, *ex ante*. There is no necessary reason why, subject to the constraints of the model, it should be possible to achieve these two objectives simultaneously by fiscal policy, or by fiscal policy in combination with other policy

---

'Economic Forecasts and Policy', *Contributions to Economic Analysis*, 2nd edition, Vol. XV, Amsterdam, 1961. For an early attempt to integrate the theory of fiscal policy with the theory of economic policy, see Bent Hansen, op. cit., Chapters 1 and 2.

Schema of Theory of Fiscal Policy

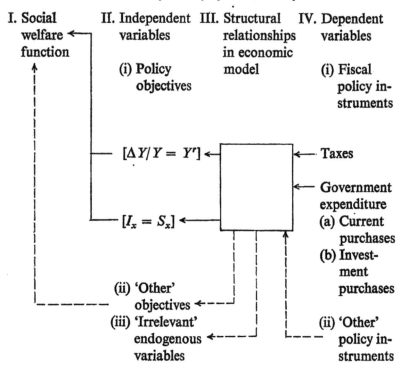

I. Social welfare function

II. Independent variables
(i) Policy objectives
(ii) 'Other' objectives
(iii) 'Irrelevant' endogenous variables

III. Structural relationships in economic model

IV. Dependent variables
(i) Fiscal policy instruments
Taxes
Government expenditure
(a) Current purchases
(b) Investment purchases
(ii) 'Other' policy instruments

$$[\Delta Y/Y = Y']$$

$$[I_x = S_x]$$

instruments. The analogy here is with a situation in which a consumer has a limited income but wishes to consume specific amounts of a range of commodities which, at given prices, would more than exhaust the income available. To reach the optimal position consistent with limited income, the consumer must decide, in the light of his preference system, what amounts of which commodities he will be prepared to give up. There is no particular reason why he should just give up consuming one commodity altogether.

Similarly, if both the community targets cannot be achieved simultaneously, there is no particular reason why the 'next best' position is to achieve one at the expense of the other. The 'next best' situation may be one in which, for example, the community may prefer a slightly lower rate of growth and full employment with some rise in prices, rather than full employment without inflation and an even lower rate of growth. In other words, we must specify the preference function of the community which depicts the 'trade-off' between growth and stability. This is the essential difference between the Tinbergen approach, which concentrates on target values of policy objectives, and the Theil approach which explores the possibility of 'trade-off'.

VIII. THE MATHEMATICAL CONTENT OF THIS VOLUME

One of the main attractions of simple macroeconomic models lies in the fact that they can be expressed in very simple linear algebra. Taking account of the extensions of these models which are necessary for our purpose means that this volume must embrace a much wider and somewhat more difficult mathematical analysis. So far as possible, we have tried in this volume to proceed from the simpler mathematics to the more complex forms alongside the development from the simple Keynesian models to their more realistic counterparts. The standard of mathematics presupposed is no more than that commonly expected of students specializing in economics at the undergraduate level (8).

One complication resulting from the extension of the mathematical analysis of fiscal policy is that more symbols must be used. So far as possible, we have tried to assign the common definition to a symbol used in economic analysis, and to economize in the use of symbols by the use of superscripts and subscripts. For example, Y is defined as Gross National Product in real terms, Y^m = Gross National Product or Income in money terms, Y^r = the 'required' or equilibrium growth of GNP, Y^d = disposable income, Y_b^d = disposable income of country B, and so on. Capital Roman letters, so far as possible, are used for aggregates, lower case Greek letters for constants and lower case Roman letters for coefficients, functional

---

(8) The student will learn all the mathematics he needs from two texts. The first is G. C. Archibald and R. Lipsey, *A Mathematical Treatment of Economics*, 1967. This excellent book has one major omission: matrix algebra. The missing field is ably dealt with in M. H. Peston, *Elementary Matrices for Economics*, 1969.

relationships and ratios. The reader must face the fact, however, that in order to provide a consistent definition of a symbol throughout the book, consistency must be traded off against proliferation of symbols. In order to assist the reader, a comprehensive list of symbols and their definitions together with an explanation of their use is given at the end of the volume.

Chapter II

THE STATIC THEORY OF FISCAL
POLICY: CLOSED ECONOMY

I. INTRODUCTION

In the present chapter we will review familiar concepts of national income determination and then extend the analysis to consider the implications for government tax and expenditure programmes. Throughout, we will maintain the assumption of a closed economy— an important qualification which does not, however, preclude the possibility of reaching meaningful policy conclusions. This restrictive assumption will be dispensed with in Chapter III. For this initial first step into fiscal policy we will find that we need no more technique than elementary linear algebra and simple differentiation.

II. SIMPLE NATIONAL INCOME MODELS

The simplest model of national income determination is the Keynesian case which assumes a closed economy and postulates the absence of a government sector. At first glance, the assumption of no government may appear a drastic simplification until it is remembered that government purchases may conceptually be classified into either consumption or investment spending. The more serious objection to the usefulness of the model lies in the express assumption of no external sector, for it at once removes a major constraint—the possibility of a balance of payments deficit—upon domestic economic policy-making. Such an assumption is often defended as being applicable to a country with only a small international trading sector, or in the more general case to countries where exports and imports maintain a fairly rough balance over time. However, neither situation provides an adequate justification. The comparative size of the external sector in no way provides an index of its importance in constraining domestic policy as the recent experience of the United

States indicates, whilst to postulate a model with exports and imports in balance is to expressly ignore the significance of the capital account. The only justification for ignoring the external sector is purely a pedagogical one; it is a useful first step towards the development of a comprehensive model which allows of both exports and imports and also the movement of capital in response to differing monetary conditions between countries.

Given such a model, our national income identity may accordingly be written as $Y \equiv C+I$, where the symbols represent national income, consumption and investment respectively. We shall assume that consumption is a linear function of national income so that $C = \alpha + bY$ where α is the amount consumed at zero income and b is the marginal propensity to consume. We now have two equations and three unknowns; to render the system determinate we adopt the Keynesian simplifying assumption that investment expenditures are autonomously determined so that $I = \bar{I}$. We now have our national income model (1):

$$Y = C+I$$
$$C = \alpha+bY$$
$$I = \bar{I}$$

which yields the familiar solution for the equilibrium level of national income

$$Y = \frac{\alpha+\bar{I}}{(1-b)}. \qquad . \qquad . \qquad . \qquad \text{(II.1)}$$

Three observations are in order at this point. First, whatever values are selected for α, $\bar{I}$ and b, the resulting equilibrium level of national income will always be such to generate savings equal to the volume of investment. Within this simple framework, without a governmental or external trade sector, savings are definitionally identical

---

(1) It will be noted here, and indeed throughout the volume, that we have followed the familiar short cut of obtaining the equilibrium level of national income by substituting *ex ante* relationships into an *ex post* identity. Strictly speaking, such a procedure is only permissible if we add the necessary equilibrium condition of the equality between *ex ante* and *ex post* values: in the present case, for example, that 'desired' equals actual consumption. We assume that readers of this volume will be sufficiently familiar with this distinction to permit us to avoid repetition of the required equilibrium conditions. For a particularly clear discussion of this distinction see Ackley, op. cit.

to investment spending. Secondly, it will be noted that the equilibrium level of national income is only meaningful if b is less than one. A marginal propensity to consume equal to one renders the income level indeterminate; a marginal propensity in excess of one achieves the even more absurd result that the income level becomes negative. Keynes's 'great psychological law', that when income increases consumption increases but not by as much as the increase in income, is not just an acute observation of human behaviour; it is also an essential assumption required by the theory. Finally, we should emphasize that variations in Y are to be considered indicative of changes in the level of aggregate demand and hence, of real or monetary output and employment. Thus, implicitly, we shall assume that employment is related to the income level by a production function in the form of

$$Y = Y(N)$$

where N denotes units of employment. We adopt the traditional assumptions that

$$\frac{dY}{dN} > 0$$

which gives the marginal product of labour, and further we assume

$$\frac{d^2Y}{dN^2} < 0$$

which corresponds to the classical assumption of diminishing returns. The production function is admittedly deficient to the extent that it ignores the influence of capital. Nonetheless, it is a convenient simplification and for present purposes it is sufficient for us to assume that an expansion of national income implies an increase in employment and vice versa. The model is a highly simplified one and its limitations and shortcomings as a guide to practical decision making are numerous. For our purposes it is sufficient to note that since it excludes not only government spending but government taxing as well it is not directly applicable to fiscal policy as such. Nonetheless, it is useful to examine some of the characteristics in somewhat more detail. The first thing to note is the various multipliers that one can extract from such a simple statement. The investment multiplier, for an autonomous change in investment spending is of course given by $dY/dI = 1/(1-b)$. This is identical to the consumption multiplier for an autonomous change in consumption at zero income level. With respect to the level of national income, it is immaterial whether a given change occurs in α or I; in terms of the familiar national income diagram both would lead to the same raising of the combined $C+I$ schedule (2). Thus

$$\frac{dY}{dI} = \frac{dY}{d\alpha} = \frac{1}{(1-b)}$$

However, the consumption multiplier for an autonomous change in the *marginal* propensity to consume is given by

$$\frac{dY}{db} = \frac{\alpha+I}{(1-b)^2}$$

Now this distinction between the two consumption multipliers is clearly of some significance. For without invoking the Ricardian expedient of numerical examples it is fairly clear that a comparatively small change in α will have but a limited impact upon the level of national income whereas a comparatively small change in b may have a decisive impact. Normally, government policy does not consciously seek to change the marginal propensity to consume (3). Rather, it attempts to influence the level of demand by changing the level of disposable income—that is, by provoking a movement *along* a given consumption function. However, the motives of consumer behaviour are still imperfectly understood. It may well be that government action may inadvertently influence marginal propensities—thus changing the *slope* of the consumption function and either countering or reinforcing the intended government policy. We will take up this concern with marginal propensities at a later stage when we allow for the external sector, for then we will show that a change in the direction of government trading policy—as for example joining a common market—may influence the marginal propensity to consume domestically produced goods *vis-à-vis* the marginal

(2) In terms of economic growth, however, it might make a considerable difference whether the change was in investment or consumption spending.
(3) A possible exception to this statement was the British adoption of premium bonds which presumably was an attempt to increase saving by changing both average and marginal propensities.

propensity to import. For the present, however, we will content ourselves with the observation that even an elementary model of national income determination as we have used here is capable of providing insights into possible policy action.

III. EXTENSION TO THE GOVERNMENT SECTOR

As a first step toward making the model more realistic we will now allow for the role of government. We will, however, still retain the assumption of a closed economy for the moment. Also we will make the simplifying assumptions that government expenditures are autonomous and income tax rates proportional to income. Despite the elementary nature of the model it will be found that the policy implications are considerable.

The basic national income identity is now represented by $Y \equiv C + I + G$, where the final symbol stands for government spending. Consumption will now be a linear function of income after the payment of taxes and the receipt of transfers. Thus $C = \alpha + b Y^d$ where Y^d indicates disposable income. Disposable income is given by the equation $Y^d = -\eta + (1 - t_y) Y + R$ where t_y equals the rate of income tax, R represents transfer payments and η that portion of taxation which continues even though income is zero—as for example taxes upon property. Our national income model is thus represented by the following system of equations:

$$Y = C + I + G$$
$$C = \alpha + b Y^d$$
$$Y^d = -\eta + (1 - t_y) Y + R$$
$$I = \bar{I}$$
$$G = \bar{G}$$

which yields the equation for the equilibrium level of national income as

$$Y = \frac{\alpha - \eta b + bR + \bar{I} + \bar{G}}{(1 - b + b t_y)} \qquad (\text{II}.2)$$

As before, we will examine some of the multipliers that can be obtained from the model. Initially we will assume that the rate of income taxation is zero, i.e. that all government revenue stems from, let us say, property taxation η. In this case our national income equation reduces to

$$Y = \frac{\alpha - \eta b + bR + I + G}{(1-b)} \qquad \text{(II.2.1)}$$

Now the government expenditures multiplier, for an autonomous change in government spending upon goods and services is given by $dY/dG = 1/(1-b)$. Again it will be noted that this is identical to the result obtained from an autonomous change in investment or in the constant term in the consumption function of the same amount; thus $dY/dG = dY/dI = dY/d\alpha$. For our present purposes, however, we wish to concentrate upon the government sector. Let us now examine the effect of an autonomous change in property taxation upon the level of national income. In this case
$dY/d\eta = -b/(1-b)$ which provides us with the tax multiplier. The expression is of course negative; an increase in the rate of property taxation will depress the income level and vice versa. If we now ask what is the combined effect of an equal change in both government spending and taxation, we at once have

$$dY = \frac{\partial Y}{\partial G} \cdot dG + \frac{\partial Y}{\partial \eta} \, d\eta. = \frac{1}{(1-b)} + \frac{-b}{(1-b)} = \frac{1-b}{1-b} = 1$$

This is the well-known Haavelmo-Gelting balanced budget theorem which demonstrates that an equal change in expenditures and taxes— so that the condition of the budget surplus or deficit remains unchanged—will not be neutral upon the level of national income. In the above case, the increase in the level of national income is precisely equal to the change in government spending—the multiplier is unity. This example is dependent upon the somewhat stringent assumptions of the model being observed and must for all practical policy purposes be substantially modified. Nonetheless, before proceeding to consider some of the more important modifications it is well to dwell upon the significance of this result. In the first place it provides the theoretical vindication of the annually balanced budget. Paradoxically, it is in fact the *Keynesian* justification of non-deficit finance. For, given the assumptions and limitations of the analysis, it demonstrates that it is always possible to secure the full employment level of income without incurring a budget deficit providing one is prepared to increase the size of the budget sufficiently. It is ironic that the proponents of annually balanced budgets are invariably the advocates of limiting the size of the government sector, for clearly the two diverse positions are not necessarily consistent with the maintenance of full employment income. Secondly, the argument illustrates that an increase in government spending will normally exert a more high-powered impact upon the level of national income than a comparable decrease in taxes. A government concerned with the trade-off between full employment income and budget deficit should logically favour the former alternative. However, since consumers are prone to identify more strongly with the benefits of decreased taxation than of government expenditure, a government concerned with the trade-off between deficit finance and electoral appeal may well adopt the latter alternative.

Having indicated the importance of the basic theory, let us now consider some of the more important qualifications. To begin with we must dispense with the assumption that income tax rates are zero. In this case the government expenditures multiplier becomes, $dY/dG = 1\,(1-b+bt_y)$ and the tax multiplier is now $dY/d\eta = -b/(1-b+bt_y)$ so that the combined effect of an equal change in both expenditures and property taxation is now

$$\frac{1}{(1-b+bt_y)} + \frac{-b}{(1-b+bt_y)} = \frac{1-b}{(1-b+bt_y)}$$

Accordingly, in this instance where taxes are dependent upon the level of income the balanced budget multiplier is less than unity; the higher the rate of tax the lower the value of the multiplier (4). However, one may logically raise the objection that we are no longer dealing with a balanced budget multiplier since, clearly if taxes are dependent upon income, an increase in national income will raise taxes over and above the initial indirect tax levy. The budget, if previously balanced, would now show a fiscal surplus. This raises the issue of how a balanced budget change should be defined, and in particular if induced changes in tax yields are to be taken into account. What then is the relevant time period for purposes of analysis?

---

(4) Less obviously, the multiplier will be greater the lower the value of the marginal propensity to consume and vice versa!

C

A second important modification revolves around the nature of the government spending. Thus far we have assumed that the spending has been directly incurred upon the purchase of goods and services. If, however, we were to assume that the government utilized the tax revenues to provide transfer payments to members of the population at large we would no longer be employing the government expenditures multiplier. Instead we would be using the government transfers multiplier which is $dY/dR = b/(1-b+bt_y)$. In this case, the impact of an increase in taxes matched by an equal increase in government transfer payments yields

$$dY = \frac{\partial Y}{\partial \eta} \, d\eta + \frac{\partial Y}{\partial R} \, dR = \frac{-b}{(1-b+bt_y)} + \frac{b}{(1-b+bt_y)} = 0$$

There would be no change upon the equilibrium level of national income as long as the marginal propensity to consume of the tax-payers is equal to the marginal propensity to consume of the transfer recipients. This conclusion is of course one which accords with common sense. If the government were to levy taxes on the one hand and immediately repay the proceeds to the taxpayer on the other, then ignoring administrative costs, time lags and so forth, we would expect no repercussion upon the level of national income. In practice, government expenditures encompass both purchases of goods and services and also transfer payments. Accordingly, we have two reasons for believing that the balanced budget multiplier will in fact be less than unity. First, because, as we have shown, tax receipts are normally dependent upon income levels and, secondly, because a portion of the government expenditure will exert no income generating impact.

To invoke other qualifications to the principle of the balanced budget multiplier at this stage is to go beyond the confines of the present model, but for the sake of continuity it is perhaps as well to indicate them briefly. If we drop the assumption of a closed economy, then to the extent that the government spending is used for imports the multiplier is further reduced. The greater the percentage of tax revenues utilized for imports, the smaller will be the income-generating impact. Finally, our explicit assumption that investment spending is autonomous obscures a fundamental qualification to the analysis. Investment spending may be adversely affected by the increased taxation now facing potential consumers or—and perhaps of greater importance—the increase in government spending may be directly competitive with the private-investment sector. Thus, before one can estimate the magnitude of the balanced budget multiplier one would need to know the nature of the government spending programme. The erection of pyramids upon Salisbury Plain would no doubt exert a greater income-generating impact than an equivalent expenditure which might otherwise be undertaken by the private sector. When allowance is made for all these factors, it is clear that the Haavelmo-Gelting example of a unit multiplier is but a special case. Indeed, it is perfectly possible for the multiplier effects of a balanced budget change to be actually negative. Our conclusion must be that the balanced budget multiplier is a concept to be used with caution but this is not to deny its importance to the theory of income determination or its relevance to the workings of fiscal policy.

Despite the comparative simplicity of the present model, the allowance of a government sector financed by a proportional income tax permits us to demonstrate a number of issues decidedly pertinent to fiscal policy. First of all, let us consider the principle of automatic stabilization. With a proportional income tax the multiplier for, say, an autonomous change in investment expenditures is given by $1/(1-b+bt_y)$. Without income taxation, the multiplier as we have seen is simply $1/(1-b)$. A proportional income tax, therefore, is an automatic stabilizer to the extent that it reduces the size of the multiplier. The extent that it is a stabilizing device may be estimated simply by comparing the size of the two multipliers. Thus

$$\frac{1}{(1-b)} - \frac{1}{(1-b+bt_y)} = \frac{bt_y}{(1-b)^2 + bt_y(1-b)}$$

which provides us with a measure of the proportional income tax as a stabilizing device. Clearly, the element of automatic stabilization is greater, the greater the rate of taxation; increasing the tax rate reduces the multiplier until, in the extreme case where the tax rate is 100 per cent, the multiplier is reduced to unity. Before concluding that the tax structure with the higher tax rate is preferable from the stabilization viewpoint it must be remembered that automatic stabilizers cut both ways. Decreasing the size of the multiplier reduces the effectiveness of countercyclical government spending.

The concept of an automatic stabilizer, therefore, is really something of a mixed blessing; it decreases the extent of cyclical fluctuations but it also retards the movement towards recovery.

As we have just seen, an increase in the rate of tax reduces the size of the multiplier and thereby raises the element of automatic stabilization. Since the multiplier, in this case, is given by $k = 1/(1-b+bt_y)$ the effect of a tax change may be summarized simply as

$$\frac{dk}{dt_y} = \frac{-b}{(1-b+bt_y)^2}$$

which in turn we may express as $-bk^2$. The relationship, as we would expect, is negative. An increase in the rate of income tax will, other things remaining equal, decrease the size of the multiplier. The decrease itself will be greater, the larger the marginal propensity to consume and also will be greater, the larger the size of the multiplier—providing the latter is greater than one. Since we are assuming that the values of both b and t_y fall between 0 and 1, this will always be the case. Thus, in the present case, the mathematical results would accord with our intuitive guesses.

A far less obvious conclusion to be derived from the model, however, is the impact of the change in the rate of tax upon the extent of any fiscal deficit associated with an increased government expenditure (5). An increase in government expenditure implies, *ceteris paribus*, an increase in the size of the budget deficit (or a decrease in the size of the fiscal surplus). The extent of the deficit will normally be less than the increased government expenditure, however, since the induced expansion of income will automatically generate higher tax revenues. It is for this reason that the financial costs of an investment undertaken by the government sector may justifiably be judged less than those incurred were the project to be carried out by the private sector; to a certain extent government public works will be self-financing (6). Thus we may write

$$\Delta D = \Delta G - \Delta T$$

(5) The discussion here follows closely G. C. Archibald and Richard G. Lipsey, *An Introduction to a Mathematical Treatment of Economics*, Weidenfeld & Nicolson, London, 1967, pp. 140–1.
(6) The opportunity cost, in terms of the use of scarce resources will, of course, be identical.

where D represents the budget deficit and T government tax receipts. Given a proportional income tax, t_y, ΔT is equal to $\Delta Y t_y$ and in turn ΔY will be given by $\Delta G k$ where k is the multiplier and equal in the present case to $1/(1-b+bt_y)$. Thus

$$\begin{aligned} \Delta D &= \Delta G - \Delta G k t_y \\ &= \Delta G(1 - k t_y) \end{aligned} \qquad . \qquad . \qquad (II.3)$$

What we wish to know is how will the increase in the deficit respond to a change in the rate of income taxation? The answer is by no means obvious. On the one hand, as we have already seen, an increased tax rate will limit the extent of income expansion by reducing the size of the multiplier. On the other hand, a higher tax rate will automatically raise the level of receipts from any given level of income. Which effect will predominate? What we require is the sign of $d\Delta D/dt_y$ which is given by

$$\frac{d}{dt_y} \Delta G(1 - k t_y).$$

But for the purpose of the argument we may dispense with ΔG by simply assuming it to be unity; such a procedure in no way modifies the qualitative conclusion. Thus, we take

$$\frac{d}{dt_y}(1 - k t_y) = -\left[\frac{dk}{dt_y} \cdot t_y + \frac{dt_y}{dt_y} \cdot k\right].$$

Since we already know the value of dk/dt_y to be $-bk^2$ this reduces to

$$\begin{aligned} & b t_y k^2 - k \\ &= k(b t_y k - 1) \qquad . \qquad . \qquad . \qquad (II.3.1) \end{aligned}$$

This expression is negative since we have previously assumed b to fall between the values of 0 and 1 and $k t_y$ must be less than 1 since we have previously defined the increase in the deficit as $\Delta G - \Delta G k t_y$. Thus we conclude that for any given increase in government expenditure, tax rates and increased deficits are inversely related; a raising of the tax rate reduces the extent of the higher deficit, and vice versa. This in turn implies that the enhanced revenue yield from any given income level more than offsets the decline in the value of the multiplier.

A closely related question to the above involves the effect of a change in the tax rate upon the total revenue yield. Again, there are two opposing effects to consider; the higher tax rate increases the yield from any given income level whilst at the same time reducing the level of income by lowering the value of the multiplier. Since, as we have just demonstrated in the deficit case, the higher tax rate more than offsets the decline in the multiplier, we would expect an increase in the rate of tax to increase total revenue yields. This is in fact the case as we can show simply in the following way:

$$T = t_y Y$$
$$Y = kZ$$

where we allow Z to stand for the sum of all autonomous expenditures.

$\therefore$ $$T = t_y kZ$$

and

$$\frac{dT}{dt_y} = \left[\frac{dt_y}{dt_y}.k + \frac{dk}{dt_y}.t_y\right]Z$$
$$= [k - bt_y k^2]Z$$
$$= [k(1 - bt_y k)]Z \quad . \qquad . \qquad . \qquad (\text{II.4})$$

Since we have previously found the expression $k(bt_y k - 1)$ to be negative the above will be positive for any positive value of Z. Thus, raising the tax rate will increase the revenue yield. The reader need hardly be reminded that the above analysis abstracts from any induced incentive effects. Nonetheless, this result provides an interesting contrast to the case of a sales tax. With the latter, the assumption of normally shaped demand curves leads to the conclusion that there is some effective rate of tax which serves to maximize the total revenue yield. Beyond this point, higher tax rates so depress consumption that total tax revenue falls and would ultimately decline to zero. Diagrammatically, we may express this as in Figure II.1 where tax rate t_0 maximizes tax yield. It follows that if the authorities imposing the tax have some concept of a target yield to be obtained from taxing this particular commodity they will have a choice of tax rate for any target income other than the maximum one. Thus if the target yield is OT, then either tax rate t_1 or t_2 would accomplish the objective. Which rate is chosen will depend upon whether or not consumption of the good is to be encouraged. This result stems directly from the fact that the tax yield does possess a maximum value. In contrast, in the case of an income tax—at least within the confines of the present model—no such maximum value can exist. No area of discretion exists with regard to the tax rate required to meet any given target income.

Figure II.1

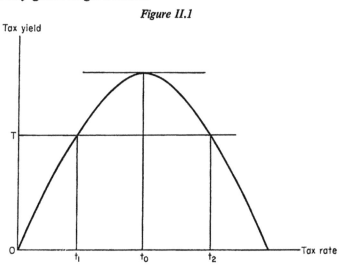

The foregoing has indicated some of the consequences of extending the simple Keynesian model to the government sector. Other implications could be derived. However, beyond a point, successive applications of similar techniques are subject to rapidly diminishing returns. For our objective is not to squeeze every last pip from each successive offering, but rather, by the gradual relinquishing of assumptions and by the extension of the analysis to other sectors, to develop a more realistic aid for the application of fiscal policy.

IV EXTENSION TO THE MONETARY SECTOR

It is not without significance that Keynes included the word Money in his title of the *General Theory*, for he wanted to show that money was important in the determination of national income. This was in sharp contrast to the classical tradition. In the classical world, money was merely a veil which one had to first penetrate before confronting the 'real forces' at work within the economy. Money had a role to play—and indeed a most significant role—in the determination of the absolute price level but it exercised no importance whatsoever in the determination of relative prices or of national output and employment. For Keynes, on the other hand, the volume of money was a major force in the determination of the rate of interest, which in turn had a crucial role in determining the volume of investment and hence of national income. In view of this, it is strange that so many expositions of the Keynesian theory of fiscal policy ignore the monetary sector. Our earlier exposition was in keeping with this recent convention. What we wish to do now is to extend our analysis to allow for the monetary factor and to indicate its importance for our generalized national-income model. In so doing, we will be taking an essential first step towards enlarging our model to include the external capital sector, for it cannot be denied that domestic interest rates exercise a profound effect upon the overall balance of payments position.

In order to introduce the monetary sector, we must first distinguish between the goods market and the money market. With regard to the former, our system of equations is virtually the same as before but now we must allow for investment spending being dependent, to some extent, upon the rate of interest. For simplicity we will assume that investment is a linear function of the rate of interest so that $I = \beta - qi$ where β is the investment demand at zero interest and i represents the rate of interest. The relation is, of course, negative. It is assumed that an increase in the rate of interest will curtail the volume of investment. Accordingly our system of equations will now be:

$$Y = C + I + G$$
$$C = \alpha + bY^d$$
$$Y^d = -\eta + (1 - t_y)Y + R$$
$$I = \beta - qi$$
$$G = \bar{G}$$

and the equilibrium level of national income will be given by the equation

$$Y = \frac{\alpha - \eta b + bR + \beta - qi + G}{(1 - b + bt_y)} \qquad . \qquad . \qquad \text{(II.5)}$$

Now, in addition to all the other variables specified before, we need to know the rate of interest in order to determine the equilibrium level of income. We can no longer determine this question without appealing to the money market. The equation specified above corresponds to the Hicks–Hansen IS function.

In order to consider the money market we shall adopt the Keynesian position that the demand for money may be broadly divided into two general categories: the transactions and precautionary demand upon the one hand and the speculative demand upon the other. The former we shall regard as being proportional to national income, the latter we shall assume to be an inverse function of the rate of interest. Thus we have

$$L = L^t + L^s$$
$$L^t = vY$$
$$L^s = \gamma - ci$$
$$\therefore \quad L = vY + \gamma - ci$$

where L^t and L^s are the transactions and speculative demand respectively, being equal to the total monetary demand L, and where γ is the amount of speculative balances held when interest rates are zero.

Equilibrium requires that the money stock, fixed exogenously by the banking sector, equals the total monetary demand so that

$$MS = vY + \gamma - ci$$

where MS represents the fixed stock of money. We can now express the above equation in terms of the rate of interest as

$$i = \frac{vY + \gamma - MS}{c}$$

which we may regard as equivalent to the Hicks–Hansen LM function.

We now have two sets of simultaneous equations which may be solved for equilibrium. From the goods market we have:

$$Y = \frac{\alpha - \eta b + bR + \beta - qi + G}{(1 - b + bt_y)}$$

and from the money market we have

$$i = \frac{vY + \gamma - MS}{c}$$

from which we may derive our solution for the equilibrium level of income as

$$Y = \frac{\alpha - \eta b + bR + \beta - q(\gamma/c - MS/c)G}{(1 - b + bt_y + [qv/c])} \qquad (II.6)$$

The above equation, which corresponds to the Hicks–Hansen solution for the equilibrium level of national income may appear somewhat complex. For our present purposes, however, it is sufficient to consider the relevant multipliers. The government expenditures multiplier is now given by

$$\frac{dY}{dG} = \frac{1}{(1 - b + bt_y + [qv/c])} \qquad (II.6.1)$$

Thus by allowing for the money market we have modified our original expenditures multiplier to the extent of the final term in the denominator qv/c. This means that an increase in government spending will normally exert less influence than before since the expansion of national income will be accompanied by increased demands for transactions cash raising the rate of interest. As long as the investment demand function is at all interest-elastic some offsetting decrease in private investment will occur (7). The same general conclusion applies to all our multipliers. For any given change in expenditures, whether by the government or the private sector, the multiplier will be less than before. Thus the monetary sector incorporates its own degree of built-in stability. With a fixed money stock, any expansion of income will be accompanied by a raising of interest rates; any decrease of income should be accompanied by a corresponding fall at least until the floor level of interest

(7) If the investment demand function were completely inelastic, then q becomes zero. In this case, investment is again autonomously determined so that $\beta = I$ and the multiplier is as before. It follows that the money market is of no significance to the equilibrium level of national income. However, we have reached the classical conclusion by invoking an investment demand function that the classical economist would hardly have considered.

rates is reached. This element of automatic monetary stability will be reinforced if price movements accompany the income change, for the transactions demand should more properly be regarded as a function of the monetary level of income. Given the institutional fact that prices tend to reveal downward inflexibility, it is reasonable to conclude that automatic monetary stability will be more potent in expansionary periods than in recession. However, the comparative strength of this factor in expansionary or contractionary periods is not our main concern. It is sufficient to note that it serves as an automatic offset to fiscal policy generally. For fiscal policy to be fully effective, therefore, it should be accompanied by monetary policy designed to neutralize the induced changes in liquidity conditions. In particular, what we wish to stress here is that to examine fiscal policy in a vacuum without regard to monetary conditions or repercussions is a procedure which may well invite serious error.

There is, however, another and perhaps more subtle reason for considering the monetary sector. Thus far we have tacitly assumed that it is possible for the government to increase its rate of expenditures without asking how such expenditures are to be financed. Clearly, this issue is of some importance, since the method of finance may reinforce or offset the expansionary effect of government expenditure. In general there are three possible methods whereby such expenditures can be financed and we list them as follows:

(a) By equal increases in tax revenues. This of course is the balanced budget change with which we are already familiar.

(b) By utilizing accumulated idle cash surpluses or printing new money. This we will refer to as the monetary expansion method.

(c) By obtaining loans from the public sector through the issue of bonds and securities—the method of debt finance.

The ultimate multiplier will incorporate not only the government expenditures multiplier, but also the subsequent changes consequent upon the method of finance. In the first case, that of a balanced budget change the multiplier is given by

$$dY = \frac{\partial Y}{\partial G} \cdot dG + \frac{\partial Y}{\partial \eta} d\eta = \frac{1-b}{(1-b+bt_y+[qv/c])} \quad . \quad \text{(II.7)}$$

assuming the tax change occurs in the autonomous component. In the second case, that of monetary expansion, the final multiplier will be

$$dY = \frac{\partial Y}{\partial G} \cdot dG + \frac{\partial Y}{\partial MS} \cdot dMS = \frac{1 + (q/c)}{(1 - b + bt_y + [qv/c])}. \quad \text{(II.8)}$$

which, as we would expect, is greater than the above. The third case is somewhat more difficult to handle (8). Since we have assumed that the speculative demand for money is an inverse function of the rate of interest, the government will only be able to induce cash holders to relinquish their liquidity if interest rates rise. The treasury must be prepared to lower the price of bonds until it has induced enough people to part with liquid funds equal to the proposed government expenditure. As a result of this open-market operation, the money supply is accordingly reduced. However, the launching of the expenditure programme immediately replenishes the money supply to its former level; no net change occurs in the volume of money in circulation and the total effect reduces to

$$\frac{dY}{dG} = \frac{1}{(1 - b + bt_y + [qv/c])} \qquad . \qquad . \qquad \text{(II.9)}$$

In comparing these methods of finance, it is clear that the monetary expansion method will be the most powerful, for in this case the expansionary effects of increased expenditure will be reinforced by induced investment from the private sector as interest rates fall. The method of debt finance will normally be the second most potent means of financing increased expenditure, although a more realistic analysis would have to allow for changes in the age profile of the outstanding debt and possible repercussions upon the lending ability of the banking sector. Within the framework of our present model, however, the only offset to the expansionary influence of increased government expenditure arises from the induced rise in interest rates as the transactions demand for money increases along with national

---

(8) Indeed, this method of finance really falls outside the scope of our analysis for in our simplified model we have omitted consideration of the bond market and the demand for assets other than money. Implicitly, we assume that the only alternative to holding money is government bonds—a simplifying assumption which permits us to bypass the complexities of the capital market.

income. Clearly, the balanced budget method is the most restrictive, for with no change in the debt or the money stock the entire burden of finance falls upon increased tax revenues with a consequent decline in consumer expenditure.

Thus, consideration of the monetary sector not only modifies our original findings by emphasizing the element of automatic monetary stability, but also highlights the importance of alternative means of finance. We will also find that the monetary sector has a vital role to play in adjustments to the international balance of payments. We will delay consideration of this issue, however, until we have examined the operation of the simple static model in an open economy which is the subject matter of the following chapter.

Chapter III

THE STATIC THEORY OF FISCAL POLICY: OPEN ECONOMY

I. INTRODUCTION

In this chapter we shall take an important step towards a more realistic framework for fiscal policy proposals by extending the analysis to the external sector. We shall find that income determination, and hence fiscal policy variables, are now interdependent as between countries. Moreover, by extending the analysis to the international trading sector we are able to consider what is perhaps the most powerful constraint upon domestic policy measures—that of the international balance of payments. We shall treat this topic in two stages: first we shall consider the balance of trade, that is the relation between exports and imports, leaving the monetary sector aside. Finally we shall complete the analysis by specifically allowing for the influence of interest rates upon international capital movements. Before concluding the static framework we will add a comment upon the multiplier analysis and discuss briefly some limitations and shortcomings of the analysis.

II. THE TWO-COUNTRY MODEL

When dealing with the external sector the first difficulty we encounter is that we can no longer consider one country in isolation. Hitherto, we have used only one national income identity; now we must be prepared to consider a series of multiple equations for each and every country entering into international trade. The complexity of the model required to approximate the conditions of the real world would be enormous; simplification is essential.

Fortunately, we can render the analysis far more tractable by assuming that there are only two countries entering into world trade. For expositional purposes this is a perfectly permissible assumption, since conceptually we can always divide the world into two trading blocs: the country under consideration and 'the rest of the world'. Moreover, such a procedure has one compelling and overriding virtue in that, when dealing with a two-country model, it is definitionally true that the imports of one are automatically equal to the exports of the other. As we shall see, this identity is of paramount importance to the analysis which follows. In addition, we can simplify the algebraic manipulation still further by dispensing with the existence of lump sum taxes (property taxation in our previous illustrations) and with government transfer payments. These aids were invoked solely to expound the balanced budget multiplier theorem, to dispense with them prevents our system of equations becoming too encumbered symbolically whilst in no way modifying the general nature of our conclusions.

We denote our two countries by the letters A and B. We now have two national income identities as follows, where the symbols X and M denote exports and imports respectively and where the subscripts refer to the country concerned:

$$Y_a \equiv C_a + I_a + G_a + X_a - M_a$$
$$Y_b \equiv C_b + I_b + G_b + X_b - M_b$$

We assume that imports into country A are a function of disposable income within country A. Thus $M_a = j_a Y_a^d$ where j_a is the marginal propensity to import of country A. For simplicity, we ignore imports at zero income. Since within our two country framework, the imports of country A are equal to the exports of country B, it follows that

$$X_b = j_a Y_a^d$$

Likewise, we may write

$$M_b = X_a = j_b Y_b^d$$

For the moment we will ignore the monetary sector. Thus our national income model for country A will be represented by the following set of equations:

$$Y_a = C_a + I_a + G_a + X_a - M_a$$
$$C_a = \alpha_a + b_a Y_a^d$$
$$Y_a^d = Y_a(1 - t_{ya})$$
$$I_a = \bar{I}_a$$
$$G_a = \bar{G}_a$$
$$X_a = j_b Y_b(1 - t_{yb})$$
$$M_a = j_a Y_a(1 - t_{ya})$$
$$Z_a = \alpha_a + \bar{I}_a + \bar{G}_a$$

Solving for Y_a provides us with the equilibrium level of national income for country A

$$Y_a = \frac{Z_a + j_b Y_b(1 - t_{yb})}{(1 - b_a + b_a t_{ya} + j_a - j_a t_{ya})} \qquad . \qquad . \qquad \text{(III.1)}$$

To simplify slightly, let us write

$$k_a = \frac{1}{(1 - b_a + b_a t_{ya} + j_a - j_a t_{ya})}$$

where k_a may be considered a 'domestic' multiplier determining the impact of any autonomous expenditure in country A in the absence of any induced foreign repercussion from country B.
Thus we now have

$$Y_a = k_a[Z_a + j_b Y_b(1 - t_{yb})] \qquad . \qquad . \qquad \text{(III.1.2)}$$

It follows that we can no longer determine the national income of country A without prior knowledge of conditions pertaining in country B (1). The income level, tax rates and marginal importing propensities of country B are all factors which enter into the national income determination of country A.

Reversal of the subscripts provides us with an identical income equation for country B and solving the two simultaneous equations yields a determinate solution for the model:

$$Y_a = \frac{k_a[Z_a + j_b k_b Z_b(1 - t_{yb})]}{1 - k_b k_a j_b j_a(1 - t_{ya} - t_{yb} + t_{ya} t_{yb})} \qquad . \qquad \text{(III.2.1)}$$

$$Y_b = \frac{k_b[Z_b + j_a k_a Z_a(1 - t_{ya})]}{1 - k_a k_b j_a j_b(1 - t_{yb} - t_{ya} + t_{yb} t_{ya})} \qquad . \qquad \text{(III.2.2)}$$

---

(1) Providing of course that the marginal importing propensity of country B is > 0 and tax rates are less than 100 per cent.

In what follows we will deal only in terms of country A but it will be appreciated that the argument is equally applicable to country B. With regard to country A, income changes are now not simply a function of changes arising internally but are also dependent upon autonomous and policy variables in country B. We may express this mathematically in terms of the total differential

$$dY_a = \frac{\partial Y_a}{\partial \theta} \cdot d\theta + \frac{\partial Y_a}{\partial \phi} \cdot d\phi \qquad . \qquad . \qquad \text{(III.3)}$$

where θ and ϕ are shift parameters encompassing all possible changes arising in the respective countries. If the level of income in country A is such that A's objective macro-function is being maximized, subject to whatever constraints exist, then the job of fiscal policy is to neutralize parameter shifts in B so that the total differential is maintained at zero. To the extent that such disturbances emanating from B are not offset by fiscal policy in A they serve as a destabilizing influence.

To bring out some of the implications in more detail, let us examine the multiplier for an autonomous change in spending in country A. In this case we have

$$\frac{\partial Y_a}{\partial Z_a} = \frac{k_a}{1 - k_b k_a j_b j_a (1 - t_{ya} - t_{yb} + t_{ya} t_{yb})} \qquad . \qquad \text{(III.4)}$$

Now if we momentarily assume the value of j_b to be zero, the multiplier is immediately reduced to k_a which is clearly less than the above for all $0 < j_b, j_a, t_{ya}, t_{yb} < 1$ (2). Thus the marginal propensity to import of country B is but one factor which magnifies the income generating impact of autonomous expenditure in country A. This is because the process of income expansion in country A induces income growth in B by stimulating the export sector of the latter. In turn higher income levels in B exert a feedback effect upon the export industries of country A. It follows that an autonomous increase in the marginal importing propensity in B will, of its own accord, exert income generating changes in country A. This issue is of some importance to the formation of common markets, since it is likely that importing propensities will increase for the member nations. The implication

(2) k_a being greater than 1 for all $0_a b <, t_{ya}, j_a < 1$.

D

that destabilizing income movements are more likely to be transmitted between the partners to an economic union may be influential in stimulating concerted stabilization policies (3). (Cf. Chapter IV.)

Other examples and implications for fiscal interdependence could be derived from the basic model. However, it is sufficient to note that extension of the analysis to the external sector modifies our earlier multiplier concepts by diminishing the size of domestic multipliers in favour of increased external impacts upon other nations. From the viewpoint of any one country experiencing autonomous income changes, the open economy appears as a stabilizer; for the rest of the world it is destabilizing. In either case, just as it is necessary to consider monetary conditions in the formulation of fiscal policies it is equally necessary to take account of the external sector.

III. THE BALANCE OF TRADE

One fundamental reason for dealing with the external sector is the fact that it brings into full conflict the choice between the maintenance of full employment income and balance of payments equilibria. We wish to highlight the conflict here by demonstrating that a country initiating an expansion of income will find the resulting increase in imports exceeding the induced increase in exports (4).

We wish to show that $(dX_a - dM_a)/dY_a$ is negative. To facilitate the exposition we shall assume that income tax rates are zero. In this case we know that

$$\frac{dM_a}{dY_a} = j_a > 0$$

and exports of country A, in equilibrium, are given by

$$X_a = j_b Y_b.$$

Thus we may write

$$X_a = j_b k_b [Z_b + j_a Y_a]$$

(3) The European Economic Community has in fact emphasized the need for concerted stabilization programmes on the part of the member states. In particular, it has called for detailed budgetary plans and economic forecasts to be submitted well in advance of actual implementation to permit co-ordinated planning. In part, this concern reflects the view that tax harmonization must inevitably limit the potential scope of independent compensatory action.

(4) For the following proof we are greatly indebted to Professor Robert W. Kilpatric of Cornell University.

and

$$\frac{dX_a}{dY_a} = \frac{j_b j_a}{(1 - b_b + j_b)}$$

since k_b now equals

$$\frac{1}{1 - b_b + j_b}$$

Both dM_a/dY_a and dX_a/dY_a are positive, the former owing to the assumption of a positive marginal importing propensity and the latter due to the element of foreign repercussion. Our concern is with the sign of

$$\frac{j_b j_a}{(1 - b_b + j_b)} - j_a$$

This we may write as

$$j_a \left(\frac{j_b}{1 - b_b + j_b} - 1 \right)$$

Now as long as $j_b/(1 - b_b + j_b) < 1$ the total expression must be negative but this will always be the case if the marginal propensity to consume in country B is less than unity for then the denominator must always exceed the numerator. Accordingly, we may conclude that domestic income expansion, will, *ceteris paribus*, always lead to a worsening of the balance of trade by generating imports in excess of the induced expansion of exports. This is a qualitative conclusion of profound importance to the theory of fiscal policy.

Paradoxically, this is a finding which has been responsible for a certain neglect of the external sector in models of national income determination. For our conclusion, that domestic income expansion leads to a deterioration of the balance of trade, would have been obtained equally well had we initially assumed exports to be exogenously determined. Such an assumption is frequently adopted when extending the Keynesian income formulation to the foreign trading sector; it permits valid qualitative conclusions to be reached and it avoids the need to consider foreign income levels and the problem of simultaneous income adjustments. For certain purposes such a procedure is entirely permissible and it is one that we ourselves shall adopt in subsequent treatments. It should always be remembered,

however, that fiscal policy effects do not heed national frontiers
and the element of repercussion can never be entirely absent. Moreover, there is a danger that single-country models may identify the
balance of trade too strongly with the balance of payments and thus
abstract entirely from international capital movements. It is to this
topic that we now turn.

IV. THE BALANCE OF PAYMENTS

In this section we make a return to the method of analysis of
Chapter II where we showed the need to integrate both commodity
and money markets to determine full equilibrium. The Hicks–
Hansen solution demonstrated the importance of the money market
in providing for an element of automatic stability. With a fixed
money stock, it was shown that an expansion of income would
automatically lead to a raising of the interest rate through the re-
newed demand for transactions balances. In Chapter II we were
concerned with the impact of higher interest rates upon the level of
domestic activity. Now, however, we wish to extend the Hicks–
Hansen analysis to allow for the external sector.

We have previously shown that an expansion of national income
will generate increased imports in excess of induced exports. This is
the balance-of-trade effect of income expansion. When considering
the balance of payments, however, we must also allow for the
capital account. The Hicks–Hansen analysis would suggest that
income expansion would aid the capital account by raising interest
rates since it is assumed that $dB^K/di > 0$ where B^K stands for the
capital account of the balance of payments. If this is the case, it
follows that we can make no definite prediction of the impact of
income expansion upon the overall balance of payments. Letting B
stand for the overall balance of payments we may express this as

$$B = X - M + B^K$$

$$\frac{dX}{dY} > 0$$

$$\frac{dM}{dY} > 0$$

$$\frac{dX - dM}{dY} < 0$$

$$\frac{dB^K}{di} > 0$$

$$\frac{dB^K}{dY} > 0$$

$$\therefore \quad \frac{dB}{dY} \lesseqgtr 0$$

Admittedly, the above analysis is decidedly partial. When considering capital movements we are more properly concerned with the differential change in interest rates between countries. Income expansion in country A will, by generating similar movements in the income level of country B, lead to a raising of interest rates in the latter country. Normally one would expect this effect to be far weaker in the country experiencing the induced impact but in the last resort the net impact will be determined by the comparative demand functions for money in the respective economies. Granted the qualification, it is still true that, just as we must consider monetary conditions in the formulation of domestic fiscal policies, so too must we take account of international capital movements when we extend the analysis to the international sector.

We can perhaps highlight the implications for the fully integrated model by invoking a diagrammatic exposition. Let us assume that initially we have balance of payments equilibria so that $B = 0$. Now if we wish to maintain equilibria upon the external account it follows that any worsening of the Balance of Trade account through domestic income expansion must be just offset by an equal improvement in the capital account via the manipulation of interest rate changes. Geometrically, we express this by the Payments function in Figure III.1 below which represents the total differential of $B = B(Y, i)$ set equal to zero. We have assumed the function to be non-linear suggesting that there is some critical range of interest rates to which capital movements are especially sensitive. The critical range, indicated by c-c' in the figure, we assume to include the 'average international rate'. The assumption is that below the critical range a raising of the domestic rate has a comparatively minor effect upon the capital account. Once the average rate is approached, however, foreign capital reacts extremely sensitively to minor interest rate changes. Above the critical range, interest-rate increases again have a negligible effect, either because all foreign capital has been absorbed or because the interest rate itself reflects a panic pre-devaluation situation.

Figure III.1

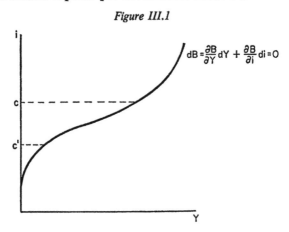

Since, for balance of payments equilibria,

$$dB = \frac{\partial B}{\partial Y}dY + \frac{\partial B}{\partial i}di = 0$$

then

$$\frac{\partial B}{\partial Y}dY = -\frac{\partial B}{\partial i}di$$

and

$$\frac{dY}{di} = -\frac{\partial B/\partial i}{\partial B/\partial Y}$$

which expresses the ratio by which income must be increased to offset a given increase in the interest rate.

For expositional purposes, however, we are currently more interested in the diagrammatic exposition. What we wish to do now is to superimpose the familiar Hicks–Hansen analysis upon Figure III.1. The Hicks–Hansen equation provides us with the simultaneous determination of interest and income, but ignores completely the question of external adjustment. It follows that there is no guarantee that the income and interest levels so determined will be consistent with the balance of payments objective. We illustrate the problem with reference to Figure III.2. We assume initially that the economy is already at full employment—the authorities having successfully manipulated the IS and LM functions to achieve this result—but that a balance of payments deficit exists. In this situation, complete

Figure III.2

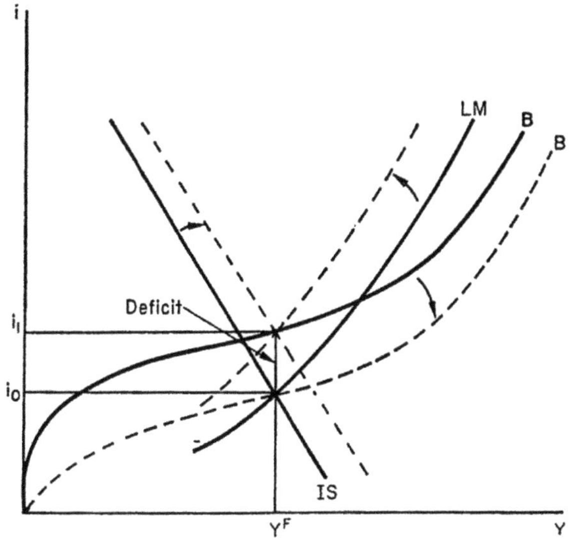

Initial situation Y^F (full employment income) with interest rate i_0. External deficit represented by $i_0 - i_1$.

Alternative Policies:

(a) Restrictive monetary policy plus expansionary fiscal policy to raise interest rates to i_1 at full employment income level.
(b) Devaluation to improve balance of trade and reconcile balance of payments equilibria with full employment at interest rate i_0.

equilibrium will only be achieved by a combined fiscal–monetary policy to offset a decrease in the money stock by increased fiscal spending. Neither monetary policy nor fiscal policy on its own is sufficient to achieve complete equilibrium. The only single instrument policy which can be completely successful in this situation would be devaluation of the currency—reflected in the downward shift of the payments function. Other examples of the combined IS–LM payments adjustment could be given but, quite apart from their purely mechanical nature, we have already demonstrated our basic point. In Chapter II we sought to emphasize the need to consider monetary conditions in evaluating fiscal policy proposals. In the present chapter we have emphasized the need to consider the external sector. A fully comprehensive fiscal policy would take account of both domestic and international money markets, as well as all foreign repercussions and induced income changes. The fiscal policy setting is that of general equilibrium. Whilst it may be conceptually convenient to ignore certain sectors or to adopt simplifying assumptions, it should never be forgotten that we have done so.

V. THE FULLY INTEGRATED MODEL

The step-by-step extension of our simple national-income model has been designed to obtain a more realistic representation of the way in which the economy actually works. We began by extending the simple Keynesian model to the government sector, and then we continued with the exercise by integrating it with the monetary sector. When we reached the external sector we dispensed with the monetary conditions to simplify the exposition—particularly when our concern was with the balance of trade. It is now time to rectify this deficiency by integrating both commodity and money market in the international theory of income determination.

At each stage of our model building the resultant changes have been reflected in a changed value of the multiplier. Clearly the multiplier is a concept of profound importance to the theory of fiscal policy; it is the valve which regulates the impact of policy action. An understanding of the forces determining the multiplier and an estimate of its size is an essential prerequisite to the construction of concrete policy proposals.

Whilst our multiplier expression has undergone considerable modification, it may be held deficient in two fundamental respects: it ignores the possibility of induced investment, and it takes a decidedly one-sided view of the government sector. With regard to investment demand we have hitherto assumed that investment spending was either autonomous or linked to the rate of interest. However, investment may also be a function of the level of income working through accelerator-type changes in the consumption level. If this is the case then conceptually we may think of our investment function as being divided into three distinct parts; an autonomous element dictated by long-term trend factors and the interest-induced and income-induced components. Thus we may write $I = \beta + \Omega Y - qi$.

The same argument applies with equal force to the government sector. Hitherto, whilst we have specifically allowed for the tax side of government activity in formulating our multiplier equation, we have assumed government expenditures to be autonomously determined. Clearly, a good deal of government expenditures—defence commitments and so forth—may indeed be considered autonomous from the viewpoint of short-run economic analysis. Yet, at the same time, it must also be admitted that a good deal of government expenditure is of a decidedly cyclical character.

Accordingly we may divide government expenditures into two component parts: the autonomous component and a component dependent upon income changes. Thus we have

$$G = H + hY$$

and

$$\frac{dG}{dY} = h$$

In completing our static framework we will take account of these refinements to the investment demand and government expenditure functions. This will allow us not only to specify the model more accurately but will also highlight some of the more significant influences determining the size of the multiplier.

Our complete set of equations for country A is now

$$Y_a = C_a + I_a + G_a + X_a - M_a$$
$$C_a = \alpha_a + b_a Y_a^d$$
$$Y_a^d = Y_a(1 - t_{ya})$$
$$I_a = \beta_a + \Omega_a Y_a - q_a i_a$$
$$G_a = H_a + h_a Y_a$$
$$X_a = j_b Y_b(1 - t_{yb})$$

$$M_a = j_a Y_a^d$$
$$Z_a = \alpha_a + \beta_a + H_a$$
$$L_a = L_a{}^t + L_a{}^s$$
$$L_a{}^t = v_a Y_a$$
$$L_a{}^s = \gamma_a - c_a i_a$$
$$MS_a = \overline{MS}_a$$

and our equilibrium level of income is given by

$$Y_a = \frac{k_a\left[Z_a - \dfrac{q_a(\gamma_a - \overline{MS}_a)}{c_a}\right] + k_a j_b\left[k_b\left(Z_b - \dfrac{q_b(\gamma_b - MS_b)}{c_b}\right)\right][1-t_{yb}]}{1 - k_a k_b j_a j_b(1 - t_{ya} - t_{yb} + t_{ya} t_{yb})}$$

where

$$k_a = \frac{1}{1 - b_a + b_a t_{ya} - \Omega_a + (q_a v_a/c_a) - h_a + j_a - j_a t_{ya}}$$

Thus, before we can obtain a determinate level of income for country A, we must first specify the conditions prevailing in economy B including those pertinent to the monetary sector. To bring out the implications more fully let us examine the impact of an increase in the stock of money in country B. In this case we have

$$\frac{\partial Y_a}{\partial MS_b} = \frac{k_a k_b j_b (q_b/c_b)(1 - t_{yb})}{1 - k_a k_b j_a j_b(1 - t_{ya} - t_{yb} + t_{ya} t_{yb})}$$

which will normally be positive for all reasonable values of k_a and k_b indicating that monetary expansion in country B will raise income levels and thus exert a feedback effect upon the export sectors of country A.

Other issues suggest themselves. We might enquire, for example, how the balance of payments would react to a change in tax rates in country B—that is we would enquire as to the sign of dB_a/dt_{yb}. However, we are unable to provide even a qualitative answer to this question within the confines of the present model. Income in both countries would decline in response to a tax increase in B and our previous analysis would suggest that the balance of trade would worsen for country A and improve for country B. However, we are unable to specify the impact upon the differential interest rates without precise knowledge of the demand for money functions in the respective economies. We therefore have no way of indicating the direction of change upon the capital account, and consequently we are unable to determine the total impact.

The great virtue of our present model is that it allows us to take account of all the influences upon the level of income direct and indirect. Consequently, the multiplier we derive from this model should provide us with a reasonable estimate of the forces determining the impact of any fiscal change. As we have previously indicated, the multiplier must be of paramount importance in the formulation of actual policy proposals.

Let us consider an autonomous change in spending in country A. In this case our multiplier is given by

$$\frac{\partial Y_a}{\partial Z_a} = \frac{k_a}{1 - k_a k_b j_a j_b (1 - t_{ya} - t_{yb} + t_{ya} t_{yb})}$$

where k_a as we have seen, is equal to

$$\frac{1}{1 - b_a + b_a t_{ya} - \Omega_a + (q_a v_a / c) - h_a + j_a - j_a t_{ya}}$$

This gives us a fairly complete specification of all the factors which may influence the impact of autonomous spending in country A. It is perhaps of interest to specify this result in greater detail. We may regard k_a as the domestic multiplier—that is the multiplier which determines the domestic impact of autonomous spending in country A in the absence of any feedback impact from country B. From the policy viewpoint, k_a is the all important variable since it is subject to direct policy control. In contrast, induced feedback from country B, whilst magnifying the total multiplier, must be considered largely autonomous; it cannot be significantly influenced by policy measures undertaken in country A.

k_a will be greater the larger:

(a) The marginal propensity to consume b_a.
(b) The induced investment coefficient, Ω_a. The more investment responds to income changes the larger will be the multiplier.
(c) The coefficient of the speculative demand for money c_a. The greater is c_a, the less will be the pressure exerted upon

interest rates for any given change in the demand for transactions cash and the greater will be the multiplier.

(d) The response of government expenditure to changing income
levels h_a.

k_a will be smaller the larger:

(a) The rate of taxation t_{ya}.
(b) The marginal propensity to import j_a.
(c) The interest–investment coefficient q_a; the greater the
sensitivity of investment to interest rate changes the greater
will be the element of automatic monetary stability deplet-
ing the value of the multiplier.
(d) The transactions demand for cash v_a. The less efficient the
usage of money—i.e. the lower the transactions velocity—
the more responsive will interest rates be to income changes
and the greater will be the element of automatic stability.

For all practical policy purposes we may equate k_a with the multiplier
when formulating fiscal policy proposals. For the sake of complete-
ness, however, it is necessary to inflate the value of k_a to take account
of inter-country interdependence as expressed in the denominator
term of equation III.4. To the extent that this expression falls between
the values of 0 and 1, the total multiplier will exceed the value indicated by k_a. Let us examine this term in greater detail. We have

$$1 - k_a k_b j_a j_b (1 - t_{ya} - t_{yb} + t_{ya} t_{yb})$$

Granted that this expression is positive, the total multiplier will be
greater the lesser its value and vice versa. Thus, it follows that the
total multiplier will be greater the larger:

(a) The value of k_a. That is the greater the value of the domestic
multiplier the greater is the induced impact upon country B
and the greater will be the feedback effect on country A.
(b) The value of k_b. The larger the value of the domestic
multiplier in country B the greater will be the response of
country B to the initial change and consequently the greater
will be the ultimate feedback effect.
(c) The value of j_a. The larger the marginal importing propen-

sity of country A the greater is the induced impact upon country B leading to a greater feedback impact. Thus, whilst the marginal propensity to import serves as a factor which diminishes the size of the domestic multiplier k_a by the same token it leads to a greater repercussion impact from country B.

(d) The value of j_b. Since the marginal propensity of country B determines the size of the repercussion impact.

The total multiplier will be smaller the larger:

(a) The rate of income tax, t_{ya}.

(b) The rate of income tax in country B t_{yb}.

All these factors combine together to modify the domestic multiplier k_a. For the most part, however, the net impact is likely to be small (5). Little is lost and great simplification is achieved by concentrating upon the domestic multiplier k_a which is directly controllable by policy action. Thus, unless specifically dealing with foreign repercussion models, when speaking of the multiplier we shall explicitly exclude the element of intercountry interdependence.

When allowance is made for all the factors which deplete the magnitude of the multiplier, it is unlikely that its value is greatly in excess of two. In particular, the post-war experience would suggest that the rate of income taxation and the extent of employment benefit and relief payments have contributed greatly to the degree of overall automatic stability within the economy.

There is, however, one difficulty in attempting any estimate of the multiplier, and that is the great uncertainty surrounding the size of the accelerator coefficient Ω. Not only is the econometric research notable for its wealth of conflicting evidence concerning the investment decision, but it also appears reasonable to assume that the accelerator will vary over the course of the trade cycle and need not be symmetrical as between the upswing and the downswing. The empirical difficulty of determining the investment function renders the size of the multiplier subject to doubt. The multiplier like so many other elementary concepts in fiscal policy must be used with caution.

---

(5) If we assume domestic multipliers of approximately 2, marginal importing propensities of, say, 0·1, and average effective tax rates of 0·25 for both countries, then the total multiplier works out at just 2·046!

VI. LIMITATIONS OF THE ANALYSIS

The foregoing analysis has outlined the nature of conventional national-income models and has indicated their relevance to fiscal policy. As a conceptual framework, the great flexibility of the Keynesian analysis, capable of almost unlimited extension, is probably unequalled as an aid to policy application. However, its great simplicity and generality provide both its strength and weaknesses. For whilst being able to offer great insight into the workings of the economy, it is equally true that it may cloak fundamental changes. Indeed, this danger must be inherent in the global construct of the model. Moreover, there is an additional danger that the facility for model building may lead to an overrating of the possibilities of stabilization policies. Accordingly, before concluding the static theory of fiscal policy it is as well to be aware of the limitations of the 'models' approach.

The first limitation of the model springs from its static nature. The type of analysis we have been pursuing in the present chapters is generally referred to as 'comparative statics'. It compares two static *equilibrium* situations in order to estimate the impact of any fiscal change. Now, the great beauty of this approach is that it eliminates by far the greater part of economic activity in order to focus solely upon stable positions of genuine interest. Without this 'simplification by elimination' it is doubtful that economics could have progressed much beyond vague empiricism. However, it must also be admitted that by expressly ignoring the movement towards stable equilibrium factors are inevitably ignored which may be decidedly pertinent to the analysis. Thus, for example, in our previous exposition there is no place for unstable expectations which in themselves may be a consequence of the transition from one equilibrium to another. Again, by ignoring the actual process of adjustment we also overlook the possibility of a change in the parameters of the model. Once dynamic factors such as these are admitted into the analysis there can be no guarantee that equilibrium will ever be attained.

Likewise, the comparative static model expressly ignores the element of time. Adjustment is assumed to be instantaneous. Clearly, however, the time factor is of profound importance since our concern is not simply adjustment *per se* but adjustment within a reasonable period of time. Indeed, the question of time may dictate the choice of policy instrument to be employed. Let us assume, for example, that a given adjustment may be secured by either a tax or expenditure change. Our balanced budget theorem has suggested that the expenditure change is generally more high-powered. Thus, if we wish to raise the volume of employment, we might opt for the expenditure change upon the ground that it will secure the desired increase in employment at a smaller cost in terms of the budget deficit. However, the expenditure change may take longer to take effect. How can we then evaluate these two policy instruments? Clearly we need some element of cost–benefit analysis able to discount the future benefits of speedier adjustment and compare to the higher deficit cost. Our static framework is completely unable to deal with such issues.

An even more serious charge has been brought against the static analysis in relation to stabilization policy. Hicks has questioned whether the static theory of fiscal policy is in any way relevant in view of the historical experience of fluctuations, all of which have occurred against a background of economic growth. In this connection we cannot do better than to quote Hicks directly:

'The cycles which have been experienced have all taken place against a background of secular expansion. Thus we know from inductive evidence, that cycles can take place against the background of a rising trend; we do not know, we can only guess, whether a stationary economy could experience similar fluctuations.' (6).

It is of course possible to allow of the influence of time by incorporating period analysis into the basic model. However, to do so is to admit of other difficulties which are not so readily soluble. It implies that we must now take account of the effects of cumulative variables which reflect the results of past variables over time. The stock of capital is clearly an example of this. Investment today may render investment tomorrow more difficult to attain. Clearly, our static model is unable to cope with this type of difficulty. Refuge may be sought in the adoption of autonomous variables but it must freely be admitted that the assumption of autonomous factors is in effect an admission of ignorance.

A further difficulty lies in the fact that the models we have enunciated above do not lend themselves readily to an analysis of price changes. Yet clearly tax-induced price changes are distinctly relevant to fiscal policy. The model we have presented does not concern itself with the price level as such. Nor does it deal specifically with excise or sales taxation, partly because of its inability to cope with the issue of absolute price levels. Yet to assume that indirect taxation as such has no relevance for fiscal policy is clearly absolute nonsense. Especially when we turn to the external account, the absence of any theory of incidence renders our previous policy statements open to grave suspicion, at least as long as the tacit assumption continues to be that of fixed exchange rates.

Finally, mention may be made of the fact that any aggregate model obscures possible differences between various sectors. Thus, for example, consumption or importing propensities may differ between households, business firms and government sectors. To take a global view involves, in effect, adopting a parameter which represents a weighted average for the various sectors. Logically, this procedure is perfectly acceptable until it is remembered that macroeconomic adjustment may involve distributional changes. Accordingly, even though we may be justified in assuming that our behavioural parameters are stable in themselves, the parameters incorporated in the model may alter owing to the revised weighting given to the sectors. To allow for considerations of this kind is of course to disaggregate the model.

Our conclusion must be that, whilst the simple static framework is conceptually essential to the understanding of fiscal problems, it is insufficient to provide specific policy solutions. The following chapters will attempt to remedy this defect. We will attempt to generalize the relevance of the theoretical framework by disaggregating the analysis and allowing for price changes. Finally, we will complete the formal apparatus by dispensing with the static framework and moving into the dynamic area of economic growth.

Chapter IV

DISAGGREGATED MODELS WITH BUDGET TRANSACTIONS

I. INTRODUCTION

So far, the reader with even a general acquaintance with multiplier analysis will have been able to deduce that the effects of any budgetary change on the economy depends on the nature of the economy which is described in the relevant model and the particular fiscal parameter which is altered in response to some conscious act of the government or its advisers. Further, even minor concessions to reality, such as the recognition of the difference between government expenditure on goods and services and transfers, affect the final result considerably if we compare, £ for £, an alteration in one form of expenditure as against another.

In Chapter III, also, we attempted to make the basic model gradually more realistic by 'widening' the scope of the equations it contained. Generally speaking, this was done by adding to the number of terms in the equation, as we allowed for a larger number of decision-makers whose transactions affect the economy's national income. In this chapter we continue this process by what may be described as a 'deepening' process, by the *disaggregation* of the terms in the equations in some meaningful way, rather than by adding to the number of new kinds of transactions.

Why 'deepening' may be interesting can be explained by two concrete examples, which are special cases of the analysis developed below. Assume that a government decides to cut its defence expenditure but to maintain the same level of government expenditure, perhaps by increasing its expenditure on other goods and services, e.g. welfare services. Our previous analysis would suggest that nothing would happen in the economy, and, in particular, that national income would remain constant. This result would be consistent with a situation in which the purchases by the government in order to supply the extra welfare services were exactly the same as those previously used to supply that segment of defence which is now cut. This, however, seems a doubtful proposition, to say the least. Soldiers cannot become, say, teachers, and guns cannot be beaten into steel girders for hospitals, overnight. A more graphic example is suggested when direct government expenditure on military officers stationed abroad is cut back, and replaced by direct expenditure on services of welfare officers at home. Clearly, this change represents an autonomous shift in the country's marginal propensity to import (cf. Chapter III, Section A), which, as we know already, will alter the level of national income. In short, changing the *composition* of government purchases may produce multiplier effects (as measured in currency units), as well as merely altering their *size*.

Another example is an extension of our international model, but applied in this chapter in an inter-regional setting. Consider a situation where a central government decides to create employment opportunities in a particular region (A) of a country because it has an unemployment percentage well above the average. Let us assume that it sets up a state-owned factory. The first round effect, an increase in local employment, will result in local incomes rising. However, the newly employed may purchase goods from 'abroad', the other regions, thus increasing further employment opportunities in other regions, which, in turn, may have a 'repercussive' effect on region A, as those in other regions increase their purchases from 'abroad'. In short, the *relative* employment and income effects cannot be judged simply from the 'first round' improvements resulting from the new opportunities in region A. This is because there is a 'spillover' to other regions similar to the one briefly discussed in our international trade model in Chapter III, Section A.

It turns out that both these examples can be illustrated in more detail by the employment of the same technique—the matrix multiplier. As this last term suggests, the mathematical basis of this chapter is simple matrix algebra—'simple' because we can make the main points by the use of a 2-sector model. The model can be generalized, but we have not thought it necessary at this stage to sacrifice simplicity for elegance (1).

---

(1) For the use of matrix algebra in macroeconomics see Peston, op cit., and Edward Ames, *Income and Wealth*, 1969, especially Chapter 2.

II. EXAMPLE 1: FISCAL POLICY AND THE COMPOSITION OF
GOVERNMENT DEMAND

In order to examine more closely the stabilization effects of changes
in the composition of government expenditure, it may be useful
first of all to describe the accounting basis of the model which is a
simple set of national-income accounts embodying inter-industry
payments (see Table IV.1). Industries sell output to final buyers at

Table IV.1. *Accounting Structure for Fiscal Policy Model* (*Input–Output Flow Table*)

Payments / Receipts	Industries		FINAL OUTPUT				
	A	B	Private con-sumption	Govern-ment	Private Invest-ment	Exports	Total output
INDUSTRIES A	—	a_{12}	C^A	G^A	I^A	X^A	V^A
B	a_{21}	—	C^B	G^B	I^B	X^B	V^B
FINAL INPUT Imports	M^A	M^B	—	—	—	—	—
Taxes on expenditure	T_t^A	T_t^B					
Incomes (including profits) (a) Taxes on income and profits	T_y^A	T_y^B					
(b) Disposable income	$Y^{d.A}$	$Y^{d.B}$					
TOTAL INPUT	V^A	V^B					

home and abroad and to each other. They purchase material inputs
from each other and from abroad and the services of factors to
whom incomes are paid. They are also responsible for payment of
taxes on expenditure and profits taxes to government.

The accounting structure governing the model has been kept as simple as possible solely for purposes of exposition, but it may be as well to consider just how far the introduction of the complications of the real world might affect the analysis:

(a) Extending the number of industrial sectors

Input–output flow tables are available for a number of countries, and may identify as many as 80 sectors, each with its pattern of purchases and sales. For purposes of statistical implementation of the model shown below, it would be difficult to justify the consolidation of inter-industry payments leaving only two industrial sectors. However, for purposes of explaining the influence of the inter-industry pattern on the level of national income and balance of payments, we can avoid the use of formal matrix algebra by identifying only two industrial sectors without reducing the number of propositions derived from the model.

(b) Extending the number of income transactions

A full national-income accounting scheme would include not only purchases and sales by sector but also transfers of income. Apart from obvious examples, such as social security benefits, transfers in the form of aid given or received may be an important item in the balance of payments and in the government account. Again, whereas statistical implementation would require some estimates of the relative magnitudes of these transactions, the inclusion of transfers in the model would not add very much to our understanding of the impact of the budget on the national income. So far as internal transfers are concerned, the normal assumptions used in Keynesian models, as we have observed, mean simply regarding transfers as negative direct taxes. Further, government transfers abroad have clearly no direct impact on the national income and have a direct impact on the balance of payments equal only to the amount of transfer. Analytically, therefore, they are not very interesting.

(c) Distinguishing national and domestic income and expenditure

It may be important, in examining both the direct and indirect effects of government budget transactions on the national income, to distinguish between foreign residents and firms and nationals. For example, if a foreign-owned firm pays its taxes in foreign currency, this will improve the balance of payments, but may not result in a reduction in *domestic* spending by the firm or its employees. To take another example, governments may also obtain receipts from sales of goods and services to foreign-held bases as in NATO countries. This appears as a positive item on the balance of payments, but, unlike direct exports of goods and services which are reflected in income payments to nationals, there is no multiplier effect unless account is taken of consequential budget changes. In any case there is no reason to suppose that the multiplier effect will be the same, £ for £, as for the case of direct exports.

(d) Identifying all relevant government transactions

A simple comparison of this account with its counterpart in the actual national income accounts issued by governments would demonstrate that Table IV.1 records the bare minimum of transactions. It also leaves open the further question of the definition of 'government'. Assuming that the reasons for not considering transfers are plausible, then this would justify leaving out one major item on the expenditure side. On the receipts side, there may be a variety of levies, such as fees and fines, and other receipts, such as interest and dividends and rental income. One reasonable justification for omitting them is that they are not so likely to be used as policy parameters for controlling aggregate demand as are the items recorded in Table IV.1.

The question of the definition of government is also important. A model which includes all layers of government must take account of the fact that the 'objective function' of each layer may differ, as will the constraints on action.

If it is considered reasonable to operate within the restrictions imposed by the accounting structure, we can derive from it the following identities from Table IV.1 which are used in later analysis:

$$\left.\begin{array}{l} V^A \equiv a_{12} + C^A + G_h{}^A + I^A + X^A \equiv a_{21} + M^A + T_i{}^A + \left[T_y{}^A + Y^{d.A}\right] \\ V^B \equiv a_{21} + C^B - G_h{}^B + I^B + X^B \equiv a_{12} + M^B + T_i{}^B + \left[T_y{}^B + Y^{d.B}\right] \end{array}\right\} \text{(IV.1)}$$

If we consolidate the two industrial sectors, the inter-industry payments disappear, and we obtain the national income *at factor cost* defined in the following way:

$$Y \equiv C + I + G + (X - M) - T_i$$

where
$$Y \equiv T_y^A + T_y^B + Y^{d.B} + Y^{d.A}$$
$$C \equiv C^A + C^B, \quad I \equiv I^A + I^B, \quad X \equiv X^A + X^B, \quad G \equiv G_h^A + G_h^A,$$
$$M \equiv M^A + M^B, T_i \equiv T_i^A + T_i^B$$

(e) The model

We are now in a position to consider the effect of a change in the composition of government demand for goods and services by turning our identities into models by the adoption of suitable assumptions

Table IV.2. *Effects of Change in Composition of Government Expenditure*

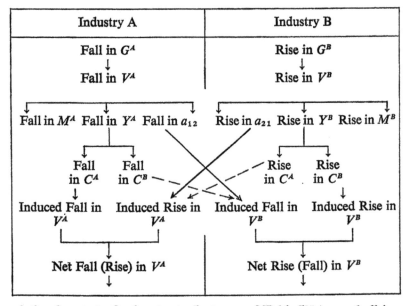

relating inputs to final outputs. In terms of Table IV.1, we shall investigate the case in which G does not alter, but its composition does.

Before presenting the formal model, it may be useful to examine the chain reaction produced by the change in composition of government demand by the use of a simple diagram (see Table IV.2). (Y is substituted for disposable income and direct taxes, and it is assumed that a fall [rise] in income generated in one sector will reduce [increase] consumption demand for products of both industries, i.e. income elasticities of demand for V^A and V^B are both positive.)

A change in composition of government home demand in the standard Keynesian model produces no induced change either in income or in the balance of payments. The simplest step imaginable in decomposing the model—two interdependent industrial sectors— produces a quite different result. Whether or not the resultant changes shown in the chain reaction are significant will depend upon the value of the import, consumption and 'inter-industry' coefficients. Thus even if the import coefficients and the consumption coefficients for each industry were the same, the net change would not be zero if the inter-industry coefficients differed.

Turning to the elaboration of the model, certain simplifications are made. We neglect taxes on expenditure and assume that all income is distributed so that disposable income derived from industry A is $Y^A(1-t_y)$ and similarly for industry B.

$$V^A \equiv Z^A + C^A + a_{12}$$
$$\equiv Y^A + M^A + a_{21}$$

where $\quad Z^A \equiv X^A + I^A + G^A$

$$V^B \equiv Z^B + C^B + a_{21}$$
$$\equiv Y^B + M^B + a_{12}$$

where $\quad Z^B \equiv X^B + I^B + C^B$

Several of the assumptions are taken over from previous models and the postulate of linearity in all functions fits well with the Leontieff-type input–output system. One case deserves special mention. The feedback from changes in Y^A and Y^B requires that an extra assumption has to be made about the split in the resultant change in consumption between C^A and C^B. Again linearity is conveniently adopted so that any change in total income ($Y^A + Y^B$) does not change the proportion of consumption expenditure ($C^A + C^B$) between industries A and B.

Using linearity assumptions

$$C^A = \sigma_1(Y^A + Y^B)(1-t_y)$$
σ_1 = proportion of total income spent on A for consumption purposes
$\therefore$ $(1-\sigma_1)$ = proportion of total income spent on B for consumption purposes.

Therefore

$$C^A = b\sigma[\omega^A . V^A + \omega^B V^B](1-t_y)$$
ω^A, ω^B = proportion of total input V^A and V^B respectively devoted to income purposes.
b = consumption coefficient
$\therefore$ $C^B = b(1-\sigma)[\omega^A . V^A + \omega^B V^B](1-t_y)$

There is one further step before we construct our model. It is assumed that the inter-industry coefficients are fixed, so that

$$a_{12} = \omega_1{}^B V^B, \qquad a_{21} = \omega_2{}^A V^A$$

Then

$$\left.\begin{array}{l} V^A = Z^A . \dfrac{1}{k_1{}^A} + V^B . \dfrac{k_2{}^A}{k_1{}^A} \\[3mm] V^B = Z^B . \dfrac{1}{k_1{}^B} + V^A . \dfrac{k_2{}^B}{k_1{}^B} \end{array}\right\} \qquad . \qquad . \qquad \text{(IV.2)}$$

where

$$k_1{}^A = [1 - b\sigma\omega^A(1-t_y)]$$
$$k_2{}^A = [b\sigma\omega^B(1-t_y) + \omega_1{}^B]$$
$$k_1{}^B = [1 - \sigma . \omega^B(1-t_y)(1-b)]$$
$$k_2{}^B = [\sigma . \omega^A(1-t_y)(1-b) + \omega_2{}^A]$$

This set of simultaneous equations could easily be solved by the usual methods, but we propose to employ now and later in this volume the very versatile tool of matrix algebra, which is increasingly being used in economic analysis.

Thus, expression IV.2 in matrix form becomes

$$\begin{bmatrix} 1 & -\dfrac{k_2{}^A}{k_1{}^A} \\[4mm] -\dfrac{k_2{}^B}{k_1{}^B} & 1 \end{bmatrix} \begin{bmatrix} V^A \\[4mm] V^B \end{bmatrix} = \begin{bmatrix} Z^A . \dfrac{1}{k_1{}^A} \\[4mm] Z^B . \dfrac{1}{k_1{}^B} \end{bmatrix}$$

Inverting the matrix we obtain:

$$
\begin{bmatrix} V^A \\ V^B \end{bmatrix} = \frac{1}{\Delta} \begin{bmatrix} 1 & \dfrac{k_2{}^A}{k_1{}^A} \\ \dfrac{k_2{}^B}{k_1{}^B} & 1 \end{bmatrix} \begin{bmatrix} Z^A \cdot \dfrac{1}{k_1{}^A} \\ Z^B \cdot \dfrac{1}{k_1{}^B} \end{bmatrix} \qquad \text{(IV.3)}
$$

where
$$
\Delta = 1 - \left\{ \frac{k_2{}^A}{k_1{}^A} \cdot \frac{k_2{}^B}{k_1{}^B} \right\}
$$

To explain the operation of the model, we return to our original problem of examining the effects of a change in the composition of government expenditure without a change in the total amount, i.e. $dG^A + dG^B = 0$ or $dG^A = -dG^B$. As G^A and G^B are autonomous components of Z^A and Z^B respectively, we can differentiate V^A and V^B, using expression IV.3.

$$
\therefore \qquad \frac{\partial V^A}{\partial G^B} = \frac{1}{\Delta} \cdot \frac{1}{k_1{}^A}, \qquad \frac{\partial V^B}{\partial G^A} = \frac{1}{\Delta} \cdot \frac{k_2{}^B}{k_1{}^B}
$$

$$
\frac{\partial V^A}{\partial G^B} = \frac{1}{\Delta} \cdot \frac{k_2{}^A}{k_1{}^A}, \qquad \frac{\partial V^B}{\partial G^B} = \frac{1}{\Delta} \cdot \frac{1}{k_1{}^B}
$$

As
$$
dG^A = -dG^B
$$

Then

$$
\left. \begin{aligned}
dV^A &= \frac{1}{\Delta} \cdot \left[\frac{1 - k_2{}^A}{k_1{}^A} \right] dG^A \\
dV^B &= \frac{1}{\Delta} \cdot \left[\frac{k_2{}^B - 1}{k_1{}^B} \right] dG^A
\end{aligned} \right\} \qquad . \qquad . \qquad \text{(IV.4)}
$$

What will happen to total output $(V^A + V^B)$ if G^A is increased and G^B is decreased by an equal amount? Investigating the properties of expression IV.4 we find that a change in composition of government expenditure without changing its amount, does indeed result in a change in total output and in total incomes, which represents a different result from the aggregate model used in Chapter II.

Thus with $\omega_1{}^A \neq \omega_1{}^B, \qquad \omega^A \neq \omega^B$

Then $k_2{}^A \neq k_2{}^B, \qquad k_1{}^A \neq k_1{}^A$

With $0 < b, \sigma, \omega_1{}^A, \omega_2{}^A, \omega^A, \omega^B, t_y < 0$

and so Δ is positive.

If we now apply these conditions to expression IV.3 and it follows that, given $dG^A = -dG^B$, dV^A is positive and dV^B negative, and as disposable incomes are a fixed proportion of outputs, dY^A is positive and dY^B negative. More important, it also follows from expression IV.4 that $dV^A \neq -dV^B$ and $dY^A \neq -dY^B$ (2).

Finally, as $M^A = (1 - W^A - W_1{}^B)V^A$ and $M^B = (1 - W^B - W_1{}^B)V^B$, $dM^A\uparrow$ and $dM^B\downarrow$, $dM^A \neq -dM^B$.

The 2×2 matrix has been used in order to demonstrate as simply as possible that the Keynesian-type model is incomplete. The model could obviously be improved and the solution offered for any number of sectors. Matrix multiplication is now a matter of feeding the necessary values into a programmed computer. There are copious examples of the use of input–output analysis in measuring the effects of changes in the composition of final output on the economic structure, including the changes in both the amount and composition of the balance of payments. It should be a relatively easy matter to perform the same kind of operation confining our attention to changes in fiscal parameters. It goes without saying that much depends upon the plausibility of linear relations between inputs and outputs, and upon the availability of inter-industry data. A further point worth stressing is that in developing countries, not only are the data difficult to come by and keep up-to-date, but it may very well be found that the impact effects are much more important than the induced effects produced through the inter-industry network. This is because the degree of structural interdependence in the domestic economy may be relatively small compared to developed countries.

III. EXAMPLE 2: INTER-REGIONAL FISCAL POLICY (3)

In our second example, it is perhaps useful once again to preface the setting up of the model with a discussion of its accounting basis. In essence what is required is a complete set of regional social accounts embodying the budgetary transactions of both local

---

(2) The reader can check these results by inserting values for the various co-efficients.

(3) This part contains sections from a previous contribution by one of the authors. See Alan T. Peacock, 'Towards a Theory of Inter-Regional Fiscal Policy', *Public Finance*, No. 2, 1965.

(regional) governments and also the central government. Inevitably, as in the first example, simplifications are introduced in order to concentrate on essential features of the fiscal policy problems.

Even before drawing up the accounts, it is perhaps worth comparing and contrasting inter-regional with the international economic transactions. In transactions between countries, obviously values must be assigned to exports and imports of goods whether these are sales (purchases) of final output or of intermediate products. The same is true in the inter-regional case, especially as we are likely to find large variations as between regions in the value of the marginal propensity to import. In international transactions, however, it is not usual to separate out factor payments across frontiers, at least in expenditure models, mainly because the difference between national income and domestic income is commonly a small one, except in the case of developing countries. In a region, the difference between national (residential) and domestic (geographical) income could be considerable, because of the strong possibility of a frontier division between work and residence and non-resident ownership of capital. Finally, while it is possible to take account of the transactions across frontiers in an international setting, the inter-regional case presents one striking difference. Apart from the fact that the task of local (state, regional) governments may be different, regional economic conditions will also be influenced by the budgetary operations of the central (federal) government, i.e. from 'outside' the regions themselves. The parallel here in an international setting would have to be some supra-national organization with taxing, spending and borrowing powers.

A simplified set of regional accounts embodying the characteristics briefly described in the last paragraph may now be presented for one region which has payments to and from one other.

I. PRODUCTION ACCOUNT

−		+	
1. Purchases of factors in region 1	F_1	4. Sales to consumption account in region 1	C_1
2. Purchases of factors from region 2	F_{21}	5. Sales to capital account in region 1	I_1
3. Undistributed profits before tax	$S_1{}^f$	6. Sales to central government from region 1	$G_1{}^c$

		7. Sales to local government in region 1	G_1
		8. Sales of 'exports' to consumption and capital account in other regions	X_{12}
		9. Less purchases of imports from region 2	M_{21}
Domestic income	$Y_1{}^h$	Domestic expenditure	$Y_1{}^h$

II. CONSUMPTION ACCOUNT

–		+	
10. (= 4) Purchases of consumption goods	C_1	14. (= 1) Sales of factor services to region 1	F_1
11. Tax payments to local government in region 1	T_1	15. Sales of factor services to region 2	F_{12}
12. Tax payments to central government from region 1	$T_1{}^c$		
13. Saving	$S_1{}^h$		
Personal expenditure	$Y_1{}^p$	Personal income	$Y_1{}^p$

III. GOVERNMENT ACCOUNT

(a) Central Government

–		+	
16. (= 6) Purchases from region 1	$G_1{}^c$	17. (= 12) Tax payments from factors in region 1	$T_1{}^c$
		18. Surplus of taxes over expenditure in region 1	$S_1{}^c$

(b) Local Government

Region 1

–		+	
19. (= 7) Purchases from region 1	G_1	20. (= 11) Tax receipts from factors in region 1	T_1
		21. Surplus of taxes over expenditure in region 1	S_1

The simplifications in this system are legion. There are no indirect taxes and no transfer payments from government to other accounts. The different layers of government have no receipts other than taxes. It is assumed that taxes are only levied on residents so that factor income from 'abroad' is taxed but not factor income paid 'abroad'. The whole economy has no transactions with other countries. Obviously different institutional assumptions can be made with appropriate modifications in the scope and nature of the social accounting flows. However, as we shall observe, even this simple scheme coupled with simple behavioural assumptions produces complications enough in the model-building process.

From these accounts (and the implied capital and regional balance of payments account) we can arrive at some essential definitions or identities. For region 1, the domestic income and national (residential) income identities read as follows:

$$Y_1{}^h \equiv C_1 + I_1 + (G_1{}^c + G_1) + \Sigma X_{1r} - \Sigma M_{r1}$$

$$Y_1 \equiv Y_1{}^h - (\Sigma F_{r1} - \Sigma F_{1r})$$

$$(X_{rr} \equiv 0, \ M_{rr} \equiv 0, \ F_{rr} \equiv 0)$$

Re-writing the identities for n regions, we obtain:

$$\sum_{i=1}^{n} Y \equiv \sum_{r=1}^{n} [C + I + (G^c + G)] + \sum_{ir}^{nn} X_{ir} - \sum_{ir}^{nn} M_{ri} + \sum_{ir}^{nn} F_{ir} - \sum_{ir}^{nn} F_{ri}$$

With no international trade, regional exports of goods and factor services equal regional imports of goods and factor services so that the sum of residential regional income equals the sum of domestic regional income.

Using the identities in Section II and assuming once again for simplicity that we have two regions only, we must now specify the functional relationship in the economy. Simplicity also demands the use of simple post-Keynesian type linear functions although non-linearities can easily be introduced into the model.

(a) The investment functions

$$\begin{aligned} I_1 &= \bar{I}_1 + \Omega_1 (1 - t_1) Y_1{}^h \\ I_2 &= \bar{I}_2 + \Omega_2 (1 - t_1) Y_2{}^h \end{aligned} \Big\}$$

$$0 < \Omega_1, \ \Omega_2, \ t_1 < 1$$

Investment is assumed to be partly autonomously determined and partly a function of undistributed profits after levying of a proportional tax which is fixed by the central government and is at the same rate in both regions (4).

(b) Government spending and tax functions

$$G_1 = \bar{G}_1 + \bar{G}_1{}^c \Big\}$$
$$G_2 = \bar{G}_2 + \bar{G}_2{}^c$$

$$T_1 = \bar{T}_1(= G_1) + t_1 Y_1{}^h \Big\}$$
$$T_2 = \bar{T}_2(= G_2) + t_1 Y_2{}^h$$

Government spending at both the national and regional level is assumed to be autonomously determined. Regional taxes are assumed to be invariant with respect to income (although paid out of income as might be the case with a property tax) but national tax yields vary with regional incomes which are all taxed at the same average rate. In addition, a balanced budget condition has been assumed at the regional government level as displayed in the tax functions.

(c) Consumption function

$$C_1 = b_1 [(1-\Omega_1 - f_{21})(1-t_1)] Y_1^h - b_1 \cdot \bar{T}_1 + b_1 [(f_{12})(1-t_1)] Y_2^h \Big\}$$
$$C_2 = b_2 [(1-\Omega_2 - f_{12})(1-t_1)] Y_2^h - b_2 \cdot \bar{T}_2 + b_2 [(f_{21})(1-t_1)] Y_1^h$$

$$0 < b_1, b_{21}, f_{12}, f_{21} < 1$$

Consumption is assumed to be a linear function of personal income after tax which has two components: factor income (F_1) received from 'home' services, and factor income (F_{12}) received from services rendered 'abroad' (5).

---

(4) Thus we assume $S_1{}^f = g_1 Y_1{}^h$, so $S_1{}'(1-t_1) = \Omega_1(1-t_1)Y_1{}^h$; and similarly for region 2.

(5) It is assumed that firms' factor payments at home (F_1) and abroad (F_{21}), like undistributed profits, are a fixed proportion of domestic production receipts $(Y_1{}^h)$ so that if $F_{21} = f_{21} Y_1{}^h$, then $F_1 = (1-g_1-h_{21})Y_1{}^h$. It follows that $F_{12} = f_{12} Y_2{}^h$; and similarly for region 2.

(d) Export and import functions

$$M_{21} = X_{21} = j_{21}Y_1^h \Big\rbrace$$
$$M_{12} = X_{12} = j_{12}Y_2^h \Big\rbrace$$
$$0 < (j_{12}, j_{21} < 1)$$

The exports of goods of one region are the imports of the other and are assumed to be a fixed proportion of domestic production. This is a slightly different assumption from the one ordinarily used in international trade theory in which it is commonly assumed that imports are only final goods and services bought by consumers. Whichever assumption is adopted makes no difference to the later argument.

Substituting and collecting terms, we obtain the following equations with domestic and national (residential) income as dependent variables:

$$\left. \begin{aligned} Y_1^h &= Z_1 \cdot \frac{1}{k_1} + \frac{k_1'}{k_1} \cdot Y_2^h \\[2mm] Y_2^h &= Z_2 \cdot \frac{1}{k_2} + \frac{k_2'}{k_2^1} \cdot Y_1^h \end{aligned} \right\} \qquad . \qquad . \qquad \text{(IV.5)}$$

$$\left. \begin{aligned} Y_1 &= Y_1^h(1-f_{21}) + f_{12}Y_2^h \\ Y_2 &= Y_2^h(1-f_{12}) + f_{21}Y_1^h \end{aligned} \right\} \qquad . \qquad . \qquad \text{(IV.6)}$$

where

$$Z_1 = I_1 + \bar{G}_1^c + \bar{T}_1(1-b_1)$$
$$Z_2 = I_2 + \bar{G}_2^c + \bar{T}_2(1-b_2)$$
$$k_1 = 1 - [b_1(1-\Omega_1-f_{21})-\Omega_1](1-t_1) - j_{21}$$
$$k_2 = 1 - [b_2(1-\Omega_2-f_{12})-\Omega_2](1-t_1) - j_{12}$$
$$k_1' = [b_1(f_{12})(1-t_1)+j_{12}]$$
$$k_2' = [b_2(f_{21})(1-t_1)+j_{21}]$$

The expression of IV.5 in matrix form follows the same technique as in Section II of this chapter:

$$\begin{bmatrix} 1 & \dfrac{k_1'}{k_1} \\[4mm] \dfrac{k_2'}{k_2} & 1 \end{bmatrix} \begin{bmatrix} Y_1^h \\[4mm] Y_2^h \end{bmatrix} = \begin{bmatrix} Z_1/k_1 \\[4mm] Z_2/k_2 \end{bmatrix}$$

and inverting the matrix we obtain:

$$
\begin{bmatrix} Y_1{}^h \\ \\ Y_2{}^h \end{bmatrix} = \frac{1}{\Delta} \begin{bmatrix} 1 & \dfrac{k_1{}'}{k_1} \\ \\ \dfrac{k_2{}'}{k_2} & 1 \end{bmatrix} \begin{bmatrix} Z_1/k_1 \\ \\ Z_2/k_2 \end{bmatrix} . \qquad \text{(IV.7)}
$$

where the determinant

$$
\Delta = \left[1 - \left\{ \frac{k_1{}'}{k_1} \cdot \frac{k_2{}'}{k_2} \right\} \right]
$$

which, for all 'plausible' values of $k_1{}'$, k_1, $k_2{}'$, k_2 will be positive and <1 so that $1/\Delta > 1$.

Some of the properties of the model may be demonstrated by the use of a simple example. Imagine that in region 1 there is under-employment which cannot be relieved (or for policy reasons must not be relieved) by migration of labour, while in region 2 domestic output and employment are balanced at a 'satisfactory' level. Consider now what would happen if the central government decided to help region 1 by increasing aggregate demand. One method available would be to increase the value of $G_1{}^c$. The effect of such a measure on the level of domestic and residential expenditure in both areas can be determined by using equations IV.5 and IV.6, remembering that $G_1{}^c$ is a component of Z_1:

$$
dZ_1 > 0, \qquad dZ_2 = 0
$$

then

$$
\frac{\partial Y_1{}^h}{\partial Z_1} = \frac{1}{k_1} \cdot \frac{1}{\Delta}
$$

$$
\frac{\partial Y_2{}^h}{\partial Z_1} = \frac{k_2{}'}{k_2} \cdot \frac{1}{k_1} \cdot \frac{1}{\Delta}
$$

and substituting in (IV.6):

$$
\frac{\partial Y_1}{\partial Z_1} = \frac{1}{k_1} \cdot \frac{1}{\Delta} \left[(1 - f_{21}) + \left(\frac{k_2{}'}{k_2} \cdot f_{12} \right) \right]
$$

$$
\frac{\partial Y_2}{\partial Z_2} = \frac{1}{k_1} \cdot \frac{1}{\Delta} \left[\frac{k_2{}'}{k_2} (1 - f_{12}) + f_{21} \right]
$$

This means that the multiplier effect of the increase in $G_1{}^c$ not only increases $Y_1{}^h$ and Y_1 but also $Y_2{}^h$ and Y_2 through the increase in demand for both factor services and imports from region 2. In addition, as well as the initial domestic multiplier effect represented by $1/k_1$, there is a further increase in $Y_1{}^h$ produced by the effect of the induced increase in $Y_2{}^h$ on the demand for factor services and imports from region 1, as represented by the further multiplier $1/\Delta$. The increase in $Y_2{}^h$ will always be less than the increase in D_1 so long as $k_2'/k_2 < 1$; and it is intuitively obvious from the expanded versions of k_1, k_2 and k_1' and k_2' above that this will be the 'normal' case.

The policy problem posed by this example is rather interesting. An attempt to increase aggregate demand in one area causes 'inflation' in another. This may not be reflected in a fall in real incomes in region 2, for this will depend upon the direction of the pressures of local demand and in a country without overt tariff or customs barriers the effect of a localized increase in expenditure may be diffused throughout the whole economy through price as well as income changes. If this happens to be the case, then there is little incentive at the regional level to take offsetting action by reducing aggregate demand, for example by reducing regional government expenditure (e.g. G_2). The most likely reaction to a rise in income levels of regional governments will be to increase taxes and expenditure, which, given our admittedly restrictive assumptions, will have a positive multiplier effect (as $\bar{G}_2 = \bar{T}_2$).

In theory, offsetting action in region 2 could be produced by increasing central-government tax rates in that region. Such a policy would be self-defeating. Factors could change their place of residence to region 1 while still working in region 2, provided that transport costs were not too high. The political objections to differential national tax rates for those in similar economic circumstances are obvious. The only way in which the national government can ensure some measure of control over 'spillover' effects of the kind described is through the taxes which are progressive with income. Assuming that the 'high' employment area, region 2, has higher per capita income levels than the 'low' employment area, region 1, then some of the 'spillover' effects will be offset by the automatic stabilizing properties of the progressive tax schedules for the nation as a whole.

F

It is tempting to explore other examples and to vary the assumptions of the model to allow for other behavioural and institutional assumptions, but our present purpose is only to present a theoretical framework and not an exhaustive analysis of all possible situations. However, a word might be said about the extension of the analysis to international economic integration. The Action Programme of the Community for the Second Stage (EEC Commission, 1962) looked forward to a situation in EEC in which commodity trade barriers, excluding agricultural products, would be removed, there would be no impediments to capital and labour movements and fixed exchange rates. Under these conditions, what happens if a country decides to attempt to get rid of unemployment by, say, a public works policy while other members of the Community have no such problem? Unlike a region, an individual country in EEC would still have control over money supply and could finance an increase in government expenditure without recourse to the capital market. On the other hand, there is no supra-national fiscal authority with powers analogous to those granted to central governments within a country. The effects of a unilateral expansion of government expenditure financed by 'note-printing' in one country on the other countries obviously depends on the 'openness' of the economy in which the fiscal action is being taken, but clearly an individual country in a Community such as EEC with no hindrance to factor and goods mobility and fixed exchange rates may export 'spillover' effects through an expansionist policy which present policy difficulties to the other members.

One disciplining force operating on the country running the government deficit will be the possibility of a balance of payments deficit which makes it more difficult to maintain a fixed exchange rate. If this force were not sufficient to prevent the initiation of an expansionary movement, then there appear to be two alternatives. The first would be to develop a supra-national fiscal authority with all the main attributes of a central-government fiscal authority; it is reasonable to assume that this would only be possible in the very long run. The second would be to strike a 'bargain' between members of the Community which would permit governments to run deficits to promote internal expansion, but only if these were financed by the issue of securities sold in the Community capital market.

As in Section II of this chapter, we have not reached much

further than the point of departure for a full treatment of the subject. A 'general' model would investigate the situation with 'n' regions where $n > 2$. A simple expenditure model has been used, but already neo-Keynesian analysis has rejected any simple linear relationship between changes in aggregate expenditure and employment. The problem of maintaining economic stability is not simply one of adjusting aggregate demand to achieve a unique full-employment level of income and employment, as modern growth theory building on the theory of income determination demonstrates. These important qualifications are considered in later chapters.

Chapter V

FISCAL POLICY, EMPLOYMENT AND THE PRICE LEVEL

I. INTRODUCTION

In the previous analysis, stabilization policy has been taken to mean the exercise of control over the level of national expenditure (or aggregate demand) and over the balance of payments, i.e. the attainment of specific values of Y and $(X-M)$. However, this definition of stabilization is hardly satisfactory. What stabilization means to politicians and to the ordinary public is control over employment conditions and over the general price level, for these factors have the most direct economic influence on community well-being. (For the moment we do not consider the community interest in achieving a satisfactory level of economic growth.) An examination of contemporary policy discussion in developed countries would confirm that one of the main themes is the problem of combining high and stable levels of employment with a stable or gently rising price level. We consider this important problem of 'trade-off' between these two objectives or stabilization policy in Section III below, but for the moment it is clearly important to investigate how we can extend our analysis to trace the connexion between changes in aggregate demand and changes in output, employment and prices.

A simple way of showing the link can now be demonstrated. Let us assume that the economy consists of a large number of identical firms producing under conditions of pure competition and interested in maximizing profits. This enables us to consider conditions in one firm as representative of production relations in the whole economy.

The profit-maximizing condition of the firm is

$$P_j = \frac{w}{f'(N)} \qquad \cdot \qquad \cdot \qquad \cdot \qquad \text{(V.1a)}$$

or

$$\frac{w}{P_j} = f'(N) \qquad . \qquad . \qquad . \qquad \text{(V.1b)}$$

where P_j = market price of the product of the jth firm

w = wage rate (taken as given)

$f'(N)$ = marginal product of labour, N being the volume of employment.

The fraction of total revenue paid to wage-earners is defined as wN/P_jQ_j, that is to say, the total wage bill divided by the total revenue, Q_j being the quantity of product produced by the jth firm. Now multiply both sides of equation V.1 by N/Q_j, i.e. the reciprocal of the average product of labour, and we have

$$\frac{wN_j}{P_jQ_j} = \frac{f'(N_j)}{Q_j} \cdot N_j \qquad . \qquad . \qquad . \qquad \text{(V.2a)}$$

Calling N_j^a the average product of labour = Q_j/N_j, then rearrangement of terms gives us

$$\frac{P_jQ_j}{wN_j} = \frac{N_j^a}{f'(N_j)} \qquad . \qquad . \qquad . \qquad \text{(V.2b)}$$

For the whole economy this may be written as

$$\frac{PQ}{wN} = \sum_{j=a}^{n} \frac{P_jQ_j}{PQ} \frac{N_j^a}{f'(N_j)} \qquad . \qquad . \qquad \text{(V.3)}$$

where PQ is the total revenue of n industries.

For simplicity, let us drop the subscript i and, ignoring summation terms, we shall represent the situation in the whole economy as

$$\frac{PQ}{Nw} = \frac{N^a}{f'(N)}$$

It follows from this expression that the level of employment is a function of aggregate demand, the ratio of marginal product to average product of labour, and the wage rate, for

$$N = (PQ)\left(\frac{f'(N)}{N^a}\right)\left(\frac{1}{w}\right) \qquad . \qquad . \qquad \text{(V.4)}$$

In rather *simpliste* Keynesian models, it is often assumed that changes in aggregate demand, and therefore in output, do not alter the general price level, that the marginal product of labour is equal to or greater than the average product, and that the wage rate remains constant up to the full-employment level. Making $P = 1$, and $f'(N) = N^a$, and treating $1/w$ as a constant, say ε. Then

$$N = Q \cdot \varepsilon$$

and therefore

$$\frac{dN}{dQ} = \varepsilon \qquad . \qquad . \qquad . \qquad \text{(V.5)}$$

Employment then becomes a linear function of the value of output = the value of national income, both at constant prices for $P = 1$. Further, if we still assume a constant price level, we can define the value of real output as equal to national expenditure in the following way

$$Q \equiv C + I + G \qquad . \qquad . \qquad . \qquad \text{(V.6)}$$

where all components are measured in real terms and the price level remains constant for any *changes in values* of all components. Given I, G as autonomous, consumption as a linear function of national income after tax, and the only tax as a proportional tax on income (t_y) we have

$$Q = \frac{I + G}{1 (-b1 - t_y)}$$

It follows from equation V.5 that

$$\frac{\partial N}{\partial G} = \left[\frac{1}{1 - b(1 - t_y)} \right] \cdot (\varepsilon) \qquad . \qquad . \qquad \text{(V.7)}$$

The expression in square brackets in equation V.7 is an 'employment multiplier' whose value depends on the consumption coefficient and the tax rate. Noting the restrictive assumptions already listed, the corollary to our analysis must be that the more flexible are the price level and the wage rate, the more tenuous is the relationship between budgetary changes and the level of employment.

A review of the analysis so far indicates that if the price level, P, is to be affected by budgetary action, it will only be brought about through the changes in aggregate demand, for example by raising G in the manner frequently described. So far, however, we have made no reference to the possibility of using taxes on expenditure, e.g. sales taxation, as a fiscal control, and this omission can be conveniently rectified at this juncture (1).

Consider an *ad valorem* tax on consumption goods. The imposition of such a tax as an addition to the fiscal armoury will clearly have similar (but not identical) effects to the raising of an equal yield of income taxes, by a rise in tax rates. Assuming that, for example, community spending does not alter in money terms, producers of the taxed goods will receive less than total expenditure by the amount of the consumption tax 'take'. In consequence, wages and profits will be cut back and, following this, private incomes and subsequently private consumption will fall. At less-than-full employment levels, output and employment are likely to fall and, depending on the shape of firms' marginal cost curves, prices as well. At the same time, one form of protection for producers will be to recoup their falling receipts by raising prices in response to the tax, the extent to which they will do so depending on the elasticities of demand for and supply of their product. This suggests a counter-influence on the direction of price change, although it would be difficult to offer a prediction of the final effect on the general price level without a more detailed analysis of the tax-shifting process.

If firms are producing under conditions of pure competition, the price of the product and the wage rate may be taken as given, and to this information we add a given consumption tax rate fixed by government. Our profit-maximizing condition, as found in equation V.1, has now to be modified as follows, in order to take account of the fact that the price per unit to the firm is now the market price *less* the price per unit multiplied by the tax rate, i.e.

$$P(1-t_i) = \frac{w}{f'(N)} \quad \text{or} \quad P = \frac{w}{f'(N)} \cdot \frac{1}{(1-t_i)} \quad . \qquad \text{(V.8)}$$

(1) Despite the fact that taxes on expenditure often comprise 50 per cent or more of the total tax 'take' in many countries, their place in the economic analysis of fiscal policy is often forgotten about. A partial explanation lies in some of the difficultes of introducing such taxes in conventional macroeconomic analysis, which will be manifest in the analysis which follows.

We have now identified some of the ingredients which will compose a revised model of the economy which clearly distinguishes income, output, employment and prices. In addition, we have identified a new tool of fiscal policy—a sales tax. At this stage we can now proceed to examine the properties of this model and how far it modifies or extends previous conclusions about the effects of changes in fiscal instruments.

II. A SIMPLE MODEL COMPARING THE EFFECTS OF AN INCOME TAX AND CONSUMPTION TAX ON OUTPUT, EMPLOYMENT AND PRICES

Recalling equation V.6 we define the real national product in a closed economy as

$$Q \equiv C + I + G$$

where C is real consumption by households, and I and G are investment and government expenditure on goods and services respectively, both measured in real terms. We assume the two latter to be independent of changes in income. We also assume that there are no transfer payments.

Money national product at market prices, Y, is given by

$$Y = CP^c + (I+G)P^k . \qquad . \qquad . \qquad (V.9)$$

where P^c is the price of consumption goods and P^k the price of 'capital goods' (including government purchases). If the index numbers of P^c and P^k are both chosen to equal 100 when the tax on consumption goods, t_i, is zero, and if the price of consumption goods is marked up by the amount of the tax, then

$$P^k = (1-t_i)P^c$$

Hence money national product at factor cost, Y_f^m is

$$Y_f^m = CP^c(1-t_i) + (I+G)P^k = (C+I+G)P^k = QP^k \quad (V.10)$$

and disposable income, Y^d, is

$$Y^d = (1-t_y)Y_f^m = (1-t_y)RP^k = (1-t_y)(1-t_i)QP^c$$

where t_y is the proportional income-tax rate.

Assuming that consumers do not suffer from 'money illusion', i.e. they take account of tax-induced price changes when taking consumption decisions then

$$C = \alpha + bY^d/P^c = \alpha + b(1-t_y)(1-t_i)Q \qquad . \qquad \text{(V.11)}$$

Substituting the consumption function into equation V.10, we have,

$$Q = \frac{\alpha + (I+G)}{1 - b(1-t_i)(1-t_y)} \qquad . \qquad . \qquad \text{(V.12)}$$

In the Keynesian literature on fiscal policy, the effects of a tax on consumption on macro-variables such as output, employment and consumption has been examined by making a comparison between such a tax and an income tax as anti-inflationary devices (2). If we inspect equation V.12, we would find that the change in *tax rate* (t) necessary to reduce output from Q to, say, Q_0, is the same which ever tax is used. However, the tax *yield* is not the same. With direct taxes, the yield, T_y, is $tQ_0 \cdot P^k$. Using a consumption tax, the yield, T_i, is $t \cdot CP^c = t[\alpha/1 - t + bQ_0] \cdot P^k$ on substituting from equations V.10 and V.11. It can be shown (3) that, given the 'normal' Keynesian assumption that the marginal propensity to save is less than one, then it requires a greater tax yield to reduce Q to some given level if one uses a direct tax rather than a consumption tax and, so, conversely, a given tax yield will have a greater 'deflationary impact' if levied in

---

(2) See, for example, E. Cary Brown, 'Analysis of Consumption Taxes in Terms of the Theory of Income Determination', *American Economic Review*, and R. A. Musgrave, op. cit., pp. 447–52.

(3) Hence $T_y > T_i$ if

$$tQP^k > t[\alpha(1-t) + bQ_0]P^k$$

i.e. if $(1-\alpha)(1-t)Q_0 > \alpha$

Private saving, S, is given by disposable income minus expenditure on consumption. With $t_i = 0$, one has

$$S = (1-t_y)QP^k - CP^k$$
$$= (1-\alpha)(1-t_y)QP^k - \alpha P^k$$

on substituting from IV.11 and V.12. With $t_y = 0$, one has

$$S = QP^k - CP^c$$
$$= [(1-\alpha)(1-t_i)Q - \alpha]P^k/(1-t_i)$$

In both cases it is evident that the condition for private savings to be positive is $(1-\alpha)(1-t)Q_0 > \alpha$, which is the same as the condition for $T_y > T_i$.

the form of a consumption tax. The intuitive explanation is obvious: even if a consumption tax does not lead to a substitution effect in favour of savings, its impact per pound of yield is greater because all the tax is at the expense of consumption rather than some of it serving merely to replace private by public saving. £ for £, therefore, a consumption tax is found to be 'more deflationary' than an income tax.

This conclusion, however, rests on a special set of assumptions which we have examined in Section I of this chapter. Imagine a situation in which the economy is at the full-employment level, and the expectation is that *ex-ante* aggregate demand will exceed *ex-ante* aggregate supply which is constant. With no policy intervention, and using a *simpliste* Keynesian model which ignores the monetary system, there would be a rise in prices, without a concomitant rise in employment and output. As we have demonstrated, we can cut aggregate demand by either an income tax or a consumption tax in order to prevent the price rise, but whereas a lower yield of consumption tax is necessary to achieve the given downward movement in aggregate demand, the consumption tax only achieves this result by a *once-and-for-all price rise*! This must follow from the analysis because the consumption tax is only able to bring about the cut in consumption if it is passed forward in higher prices.

Even if òne accepts that a rise in the consumption tax rate would esult in price rises lower than those which would otherwise obtain without any adjustment in tax rates, and ignores the 'double-think' surrounding the proposition that a consumption tax is 'more deflationary' although it produces a price rise, we must clearly look more closely at the effects on the analysis of relaxing the special assumptions mentioned on p. 86. It will be remembered that these assumptions enabled the simple Keynesian analysis to dispense with the consideration of the maximizing behaviour of firms and individuals, and to avoid considering what happens if there is a 'trade-off' between employment and price changes. In addition, the model does not allow any investigation of 'cost-push' inflation or the wage-price spiral, which empirical investigations have indicated as important.

The next section of this chapter attempts to combine some of the elements in Sections I and II of this chapter, but the reader is warned that one cannot take account of all the additional complications mentioned in the previous paragraph. All we can hope to do, given the constraint of space and the level of analysis of this volume, is to demonstrate in what direction modern economic analysis must move in order to examine in depth the link between output, employment, prices and the control of their movements by fiscal policy.

III. AN EXTENSION OF THE SIMPLE MODEL

It may be useful to begin by setting up our full set of equations for the extended model, before considering each one:

$$N = N(Q) \qquad . \qquad . \qquad . \qquad . \qquad \text{(V.13a)}$$

$$P^c = \frac{w}{f'(N)} \cdot \frac{1}{(1-t_i)} \qquad . \qquad . \qquad . \qquad \text{(V.13b)}$$

$$Q = C + I + G \qquad . \qquad . \qquad . \qquad \text{(V.13c)}$$

and assuming that we adopt the assumption of no money illusion in the consumption function

$$Q = \frac{\alpha + (I+G)}{1 - b(1-t_i)(1-t_y)} \qquad . \qquad . \qquad \begin{array}{c} \text{(V.14)} \\ (= \text{V.12}) \end{array}$$

Equation V.13a is a revised version of equation V.5, but we remove the strong assumption that employment is a linear function of national output. We shall assume that $dN/dQ > 0$ and $d^2N/dQ^2 > 0$. Equation V.13b is simply the alternative version of equation V.8. It will be assumed initially that the wage rate, w, is constant. It is further assumed that we are only interested in movements in the price of consumption goods, these being the only goods subject to the *ad valorem* tax of rate t_i. In equations V.13c and V.14, I is exogenously determined.

Let us now consider what the effect will be on output, employment and the price level of a change in either income tax or consumption tax, and let it be assumed that policy demands that a given change in Q is needed. If this is so, we know from previous analysis that the amount of the consumption tax needed to produce a given fall in Q is less than the amount of income tax. As Q changes by a given amount, the consequential fall in employment is the same in both cases. However, as employment will fall more rapidly than output, then the marginal product of labour will rise. This means that, with no other changes in the independent variables in equation V.13b, P^c must fall, given the profit maximization condition already considered in Section I, which led to the formulation in equation V.8. However, this fall in P^c is only consistent with the case in which we use a change in t_y, i.e. in the rate of income tax, in order to reduce Q. If we use the alternative of a rise in t_i, then clearly the price-reducing effect of the rise in labour's marginal product is offset by the rise in t_i. Whether or not P^c will rise will depend on the exact shape of the marginal product curve of labour and, of course, on the change in t_i. For any given change in t_i, the closer the marginal is to the average product of labour—as commonly found in Keynesian-type models— the greater is the likelihood of a rise in P^c.

Having proceeded this far in modifying the Keynesian analysis of income determination in order to take account of the effects of different taxes on the level of employment, output, and prices, one is tempted, like Pandora, to open the box of hidden assumptions which, once allowed to escape, destroy the simple innocence of the model presented. If we are brave enough to do this, then there are at least two major problems confronting us.

The first is whether or not it is reasonable to assume that any change in P^c will leave the level of real aggregate demand unaffected. Let us rewrite the multiplicand in equation V.14 so that $\alpha + I + G = A$. In terms of our analysis, can we assume that $dA/dP^c = 0$? There is a whole host of reasons why one may question this assumption. It would be dangerous to assume that, on balance, $dA/dP^c = 0$. On the whole, one might hazard the guess that real aggregate demand is likely, if anything, to decrease, *other things being equal* if P^c rises and vice versa if P^c falls. Consider the following four factors:

(i) *Distribution effects.* Assume that money aggregate demand remains constant, but P^c rises, then with a constant wage rate and a fall in employment, there will be a redistribution of income from wages to profits (cf. equation V.2a). The normal conclusion would be that such a redistribution, if it did not alter the value of A, would lower the value of α in equation V.14, so that real consumption demand would fall.

(ii) *Money supply exogenously determined.* Unless the supply of money is demand determined, i.e. will respond automatically to changes in money aggregate demand, a price increase will tend to reduce the liquidity of the economy, leading to higher interest rates. As we know from the analysis in Chapter II this may curtail spending.

(iii) *Substitution effects of the tax.* Whereas the assumption in the consumption function employed in equations V.11 and V.14 postulates that the consumer will raise his consumption out of a given income in order to allow for the cut in its real value by the consumption tax, other assumptions are possible. There could be a 'money illusion' in the consumption function, which would mean that consumers only maintain the money value of consumption despite the raising of prices by the consumption tax. Our consumption function has now to be rewritten as

$$CP^c = \alpha + b(Y^d) > \alpha + b(1-t_y)(1-t_i)QP^c$$

or

$$C = \alpha/P^c + b(1-t_y)(1-t_i)Q \ . \qquad . \qquad . \quad \text{(V.10a)}$$

Equation V.12 has now to be rewritten as

$$Q = \frac{\alpha/P^c + I + G}{1 - b(1-t_y)(1-t_i)} \qquad . \qquad . \quad \text{(V.12a)}$$

In short, a price increase caused by the consumption tax would reduce the constant term in the consumption function, and I and G could also decline if firms and government demand is fixed in terms of the money and not the real value of services.

(iv) *Balance of trade effect.* If prices of consumption goods rise relative to the price of competing imports, and the exchange rate is fixed, demand may be switched to purchases from foreign buyers thus reducing real demand at home.

Even if we could get away with the assumption that $dA/dP^c = 0$ and α is constant, so that the model is stable, there is still the further problem of the plausibility of the assumption that the wage rate, w, will remain constant, throughout the process of adjustment which would follow from either form of tax change. The prevailing view in economic analysis at various levels of sophistication is that w is unresponsive to a fall in the price index of consumption goods but positively related to a rise in the index. This would suggest that, in terms of our model, any rise in P^c induced by a rise in t_i, would produce a wage-price spiral. However, as we have seen, the possibility of an indefinite expansion in the level of money aggregate demand is a remote one, at least in terms of our model, so that, if P^c rose, in the longer run Q would have to fall further than the amount induced by the initial tax changes, with consequential effects on employment and P^c itself.

To build a wage-price spiral into our model, set off by a tax change which altered prices, would require two major alterations in the model's structure. In the first place, it would be necessary to 'dynamize' the model and show the period-by-period changes in the variables which interest us. Our model only portrays the conditions which produce static equilibrium in the commodity market and the labour market and equilibrium is assumed to be achieved instantaneously. Unfortunately, dynamizing such models would take us far beyond the analytical scope of this work (4). The second major alteration would be in the nature of the assumptions about economic policy. We have only examined the effects of alternative tax changes without specific reference to policy 'mixes'. Only later do we consider what happens when we build in assumptions about the *desirability* of the changes produced in output, employment and prices by fiscal action. To sustain a wage-price spiral, we would have to build in the assumption that trade unions in pressing for higher wages could reasonably expect that the 'cost' of doing so would not be an increase in unemployment of its members and therefore that employers also could reasonably hope to pass wage claims forward. In other words, offsetting adjustments would be made in variables controlled by government, e.g. the money supply, to accommodate wage earners and employers.

---

(4) For an example of an attempt to extend the analysis in this direction, see A. T. Peacock and J. Williamson, 'Consumption Taxes and Compensatory Finance', *Economic Journal*, Vol. LXXVII, March 1967. Most of this section is based on this article.

To conclude, therefore, the extension of the 'normal' Keynesian-type expenditure model to examine changes in variables other than aggregate demand is a complicated business and the reader must accept that we have only been able to scratch the surface of many of the problems encountered in approaching greater realism. At the same time, it seems better to know these difficulties exist, even if they are not surmounted, rather than to lead him astray into believing that movements in aggregate demand offer enough information about the direction of movements in prices, wages, employment and output, as the more naive Keynesian models would have us believe.

Chapter VI

FISCAL POLICY AND ECONOMIC GROWTH

I. INTRODUCTION

By extending the analysis to the sphere of economic growth, we are taking an essential step towards attaining greater realism and relevance for fiscal policy, for conclusions derived from static analysis may no longer be applicable when we permit of dynamic considerations (1). Regrettably, however, it must be conceded that the theory of fiscal policy within a dynamic setting is still very much in its infancy. Whilst much has been done in assessing the impact of tax changes upon investment incentives, saving ratios, work effort and so forth—all factors which may influence growth rates—comparatively little has been done to bring fiscal changes more formally into growth models. There appear to be two major reasons for this. First, most of the policy discussion has been concerned with specific fiscal proposals designed to influence actual short-term growth rates, whereas the greater part of growth theorizing has been concerned not with actual growth rates as such but rather with the required rates needed to fulfil certain long-term conditions. It can hardly be considered surprising if the economic policy-maker should feel somewhat remote from the concern with golden-age solutions. Secondly, and possibly of more importance, it is also the consequence of the fact that recent growth theory has developed in such a way as to render fiscal considerations virtually irrelevant to long-term growth paths. This latter development has been associated with the

---

(1) It may be shown, for example, that automatic fiscal stabilizers may actually be destabilizing when considered in a dynamic setting! Cf. D. J. Smyth, 'Can Automatic Stabilizers Be Destabilizing', *Public Finance*, 1963; and A. T. Peacock, 'Built-in Flexibility and Economic Growth', in *Stabile Preise in Wachsender Wirtschaft*, ed. Bombach, Tübingen, 1960. We will return to this issue in Chapter VII.

gradual eclipse of the Harrod–Domar model in favour of neo-classical formulations. In the former case growth rates are almost entirely determined by capital formation and fiscal policy consequently has a major role to play (2). In the neo-classical formulations, however, growth rates are wholly determined by population growth; fiscal policy may indeed be used to hasten capital formation but this results only in a changed capital–labour ratio and exerts no impact upon the long-term growth path. Fiscal policy thus becomes an irrelevancy (3).

Whilst we will critically examine this conclusion at a later stage, it remains a fact that from the practical standpoint of policy-making the existing theoretical framework of economic growth does not contribute substantially to fiscal policy. Nor is it easy to adapt the above models in order to apply them to the relevant policy issues in public finance. We are thus compelled to discuss fiscal policy for economic growth in a context which is largely divorced from the theoretical framework of growth economics. Indeed, this is one of the major contrasts between dynamic and static fiscal policy. In the latter case, the static theory of fiscal policy is a logical extension of static Keynesian theory; whereas fiscal policy for economic growth has yet to find its theoretical foundation.

II. HARROD–DOMAR GROWTH

When the Harrod–Domar model is extended to the government sector the increase in capacity income will be a function of both private investment spending and also government spending where the latter is utilized to enlarge capacity output (4). We shall assume

(2) This approach, the essence of which is the assumption of a constant capital–output ratio, is still very much in favour in discussions concerning the less advanced economies.

(3) Fiscal policy parameters have indeed been included in neo-classical growth models by a number of authors in recent years. For the most part, however, they have been concerned with distributional issues, or with the speed of adjustment to the growth path given any autonomous disturbance—and not with the underlying nature of the growth path itself. Cf. J. Cornwall, 'Three Paths to Full Employment Growth', *Quarterly Review of Economics*, February 1963; R. Sato, 'Fiscal Policy in a Neo-Classical Growth Model', *Review of Economic Studies*, February 1963; and K. Sato, Taxation and Neo-Classical Growth', *Public Finance*, No 3. 1967.

(4) Cf. R. A. Musgrave, *The Theory of Public Finance*, pp. 484 ff.

G

that the increase in capacity output in the current period n, is determined solely by the total amount of investment spending in the previous period. Thus we may write

$$\Delta Y_n^c = \sigma(I_{n-1} + pG_{n-1})$$

where Y^c denotes capacity income, the subscript n the time period involved, and p the percentage of government expenditure which is essentially of an investment character. σ is the output–capital ratio which we here assume to be identical as between the government and private sectors. Whilst this assumption may appear to be a little tenuous at first glance it is as well to note that conceptually we can always render the output–capital ratio equal between the sectors by making the corresponding adjustment in p.

Turning to the demand side of the economy, we adopt a simple Keynesian national income model expressed in monetary terms and have:

$$Y_n^m \equiv C_n^m + I_n^m + F_n^m$$

where the superscript denotes the monetary unit. Consumption we assume to be a simple function of disposable income in the current period and we make the simplifying assumption that average and marginal propensities are equal. Thus, $C_n^m = b Y_n^m (1 - t_y)$ where t_y is the rate of income tax and assumed invariant. Thus, $t_y = T_n^m / Y_n^m$ where T is the tax yield. Following Domar we take investment expenditures to be autonomously determined (5) and finally we make government expenditures a constant proportion of national income so that

$$I_n^m = I_{n-1}^m = I_n^m$$
$$G_n^m = g Y_n^m$$

Accordingly, the equilibrium level of money national income is

$$Y_n^m = \frac{I_n^m}{(1 - b + bt_y - g)}$$

---

(5) In Harrod's formulation an attempt is made to relate investment spending to income changes by invoking the accelerator principle. We will have recourse to this additional sophistication when we consider the Harrod–Domar model and automatic stabilization. See Chapter VII.

and the increase in aggregate demand resulting from an increase in the level of investment spending is

$$\Delta Y_n^m = \frac{\Delta I_n^m}{(1-b+bt_y-g)}$$

Assuming that full employment prevails initially, continued full employment of the capital stock without inflation requires that the increase in monetary demand just matches the increase in capacity income. Thus the required condition is that

$$\Delta Y_n^c = \Delta Y_n^m$$

or, alternatively,

$$\sigma(I_{n-1}+pG_{n-1}) = \frac{\Delta I_n^m}{(1-b+bt_y-g)}$$

Dividing throughout by Y_{n-1}^m we obtain

$$\frac{\Delta Y_n^m}{Y_{n-1}^m} = \frac{\sigma I_{n-1}}{Y_{n-1}^m} + \frac{\sigma p G_{n-1}}{Y_{n-1}^m} = \frac{\Delta I_n^m/(1-b+bt_y-g)}{I_{n-1}^m/(1-b+bt_y-g)}$$

But since $\dfrac{G_{n-1}}{Y_{n-1}^m} = g$, and $\dfrac{I_{n-1}}{Y_{n-1}^m}$ is simply $(1-b+bt_y-g)$ we may

express our required condition as

$$\frac{\Delta Y_n^m}{Y_{n-1}^m} = \sigma(1-b+bt_y-g+pg) = \frac{\Delta I_n^m}{I_{n-1}^m}$$

This equation postulates that the required growth of monetary aggregate demand, needed to maintain full employment of the capital stock, is equal to the required growth of monetary investment expenditures and, moreover, is itself a function of both government spending and tax changes. It follows, that if the actual growth of income falls below the required, it is possible to do one of two things: either attempt to raise the actual growth rate by a programme of investment incentives and the like, or alternatively to decrease the required growth of income by the manipulation of taxes and expenditures. Of the two, the former policy of raising actual growth rates is possibly preferable from a welfare viewpoint but perhaps also the more difficult. For, if actual growth rates lag behind the required, then excess capacity must exist and attempts to increase investment spending are hardly likely to succeed. Accordingly, it would seem more appropriate to examine the implications of varying taxes and government spending so as to influence the required rate of growth, Y^r.

An increase in the rate of taxation will raise the required rate of growth since $dY^r/dt_y = \sigma b$ and is positive in all cases where the marginal propensity to consume is positive. Likewise, an increase in the level of government spending—assuming that p remains unaltered—will normally reduce the required rate of growth since $dY^r/dg = \sigma(p-1)$ and is negative in all cases where p is less than one. More interesting, perhaps, is the case of a balanced budget change. We want to evaluate

$$\frac{\partial Y^r}{\partial t_y} \cdot dt_y + \frac{\partial Y^r}{\partial g} \cdot dg$$

where $dt_y = dg$. Thus we have

$$(\sigma b) \, dg + \sigma(p-1) \, dg$$

The resulting impact upon the required rate of growth is determined solely by the extent to which government expenditures are capacity creating. If $p = 1$, so that there is no consumption element in government expenditures, then the balanced budget change reduces to $(\sigma b)dg$ and is positive in all cases where the marginal propensity to consume is positive. Similarily, if $p = 0$, so that all government spending is of the nature of consumption, then the impact of a balanced budget change reduces to $(\sigma b - \sigma)dg$ and the required growth rate must fall. It follows that there is some value of p such as to leave the required growth rate unaffected. Our conclusion must be that, given a discrepancy between required and actual growth rates, variations in taxes and expenditures may achieve equality between the two by influencing the required growth rate. Other examples could be invoked. However, whilst of some pedagogic value in illustrating the implications of the Harrod–Domar model, it is hardly likely that the results will be of direct relevance to fiscal policy. For our concern—and indeed Harrod and Domar's initial concern—is not limited solely to attaining full employment of the capital stock. Of greater importance, perhaps, is the need to secure the full employment of the labour force. To assume that one can equate full employment of the capital stock with full employment of the labour force is a convenient assumptioh often invoked, but not one likely to enhance the status of the economics profession. Should the labour force be expanding at a faster rate than the actual growth of income, a policy of decreasing the required growth of income is tantamount to adopting a policy of perpetual unemployment. Clearly, in this situation, the need is for specific measures to raise the actual growth rate in the endeavour to attain a 'golden age' solution where actual rates, required rates and population rates are brought into equality. Regrettably, the Harrod–Domar formulation offers little in the way of a solution to this question. Our conclusion must be that from the pragmatic standpoint of fiscal policy the Harrod–Domar model offers little that is relevant.

III. THE NEO-CLASSICAL MODEL

Whilst the Harrod–Domar formulation of the growth process was undoubtedly an important conceptual extension of the Keynesian model, in retrospect it seems clear that the peculiar characteristics of the analysis sprang from the limiting and certainly questionable assumption of fixed-factor proportions. The alternative assumption, that the capital–labour ratio is variable, is the essential distinguishing feature of the neo-classical model. It follows, again in contrast to the Harrod–Domar model, that the capital–output ratio is also variable. Both these postulates rest upon a second assumption, often only implicitly stated, that entrepreneurs react to changes in comparative factor prices. If capital is expanding faster than the labour supply, for example, the rate of interest falls relative to wages and entrepreneurs are induced to adopt more capital-intensive methods. More often than not, such a behaviouristic assumption is incorporated into the analysis by invoking the mathematically convenient Cobb–Douglas production function. Now, it is clear that such a production function will minimize the role of fiscal policy, for, whilst taxes can be manipulated to increase total saving, the employment of greater capital-intensive methods of production will be accompanied by a decline in the marginal product of capital. Indeed, the fundamental conclusion of the neo-classical model is that the long-run growth rate of the economy is determined uniquely by the growth rate of population, and accordingly, fiscal policy is of no consequence (6). In what follows we will first of all examine a neo-classical growth model to derive this basic result (7). We will, however, examine the implications for fiscal policy in somewhat more detail. We may find that the scope for fiscal policy is rather less limited than hitherto supposed.

National income is assumed to consist of homogeneous commodities whose growth, ΔY, is assumed a simple function of time. Of any increment in income, a fraction s is saved, being immediately invested and the remainder consumed. Thus, we may write, $s = S/Y = I/Y$, and $1-s = C/Y$. Capital accumulation is the consequence of net investment over time. Net investment may, therefore, be defined as the growth of the capital stock with respect to time. Accordingly we have $I = sY = dK/dn = \dot{K}$ where K represents the capital stock. We now assume a production function of the following form, $Y = E(K, N)$ where N represents the labour input. It is convenient to assume that the production function is of the Cobb–Douglas variety implying constant returns to scale and diminishing returns to the input of any one factor. We also assume that labour input is growing at a constant rate ψ so that

$$N(n) = N_0 e^{\psi n}$$

where ψ is the growth rate of the population. We now have

$$\dot{K} = sY = sE(K, N) = sE(K, N_0 e^{\psi n})$$

This is a differential equation the solution of which determines the time path of capital accumulation which must be followed if all the available labour input is to be fully employed, given the nature of the production function and the saving propensity s. The next step is to introduce the notion of the capital–labour ratio r which, in sharp contrast to the Harrod–Domar model, is explicitly introduced

---

(6) Even within the confines of the neo-classical framework, this conclusion may be a little too sweeping. Growth rates are of course determined by the growth of the labour force and not by the growth of population. It is perfectly possible that fiscal policy variables may influence participation rates, for example.

(7) The simple model presented here follows closely the pioneering article by R. M. Solow, 'A Contribution to the Theory of Economic Growth', *Quarterly Journal of Economics*, February 1956.

as a variable. The fundamental assumption of the model is that changes in relative factor prices—determined by the marginal productivity doctrine—will ensure that full employment of both labour and capital is maintained. Given this basic assumption, which as we have already indicated implies an assumption about entrepreneurial behaviour, then the purpose of the neo-classical model is to show that no matter what the rate of growth of the labour force may be, there is always a time path of capital accumulation consistent with its full employment.

The capital–labour ratio r is of course K/N. The proportionate rate of change with respect to time in r, therefore, is simply equal to the proportionate rate of change in K minus the proportionate rate of change in the labour force. Hence we have

$$\frac{\dot{r}}{r} = \frac{\dot{K}}{K} - \frac{\dot{N}}{N}$$

But $\dot{N}/N$ is simply the growth rate of population ψ, and we already have $\dot{K} = sE(K, N)$. Thus we may write

$$\dot{r} = r\frac{sE(K,N)}{K} - \psi r$$

We can now make use of the assumption of a Cobb–Douglas production function. Since this exhibits constant returns to scale, it is possible to divide both factors K and N by N, providing we multiply the total function by the same amount.
Thus

$$\dot{r} = r\frac{sNE\left(\frac{K,1}{N}\right)}{K} - \psi r$$

But $K/N = r$, $N/K = 1/r$ and the total expression reduces to

$$\dot{r} = sE(r,1) - \psi r$$

This equation is of fundamental importance to the argument which follows. It may be interpreted in the following way: $E(r, 1)$ is simply the total output of one worker which varies according to the amount of capital at his disposal. It is thus output per capita as a function of capital per capita. Likewise, $sE(r, 1)$ may be considered as the amount of saving per capita expressed as a function of capital per capita. ψr may be considered as the proportionate change in the capital–labour ratio with respect to time as a consequence of population growth. Thus the total expression,

$$\dot{r} = sE(r,1) - \psi r$$

gives the rate of change in the capital–labour ratio as a function of the increase in savings per worker due to income growth and the decrease in capital per worker due to population growth. Clearly, three situations are possible:

if $\dot{r} > 0$, it implies that the increase in capital per worker due to income growth exceeds the decrease occasioned by population expansion;

and, conversely, if $\dot{r} < 0$, the capital–output ratio is declining as a consequence of population expansion running ahead of net capital formation.

The dividing case is represented by $\dot{r} = 0$, where the increased capital formation arising from income expansion is exactly offset by the force of population expansion thus maintaining the capital–labour ratio as a constant. It is precisely this case which provides the long-term equilibrium solution to the neo-classical framework. It is inherent in the neo-classical construct that whatever the initial value for $\dot{r}$ it will converge towards zero. To see this, consider the implications of $\dot{r} = 0$. If $\dot{r} > 0$ then the amount of capital per worker is increasing. But, given the assumption of a Cobb–Douglas production function, the increasing capital input will be subject to progressively diminishing returns. National income will continue to grow, but at an ever-decreasing rate. With a constant savings ratio, it follows that savings will also continue to grow but at an ever-decreasing rate. Meanwhile population continues to expand at an exogenously determined rate. Thus, although initially savings were outstripping the growth of population, leading to a rising capital–labour ratio, the combination of a declining rate of change in savings growth together with a constant rate of change in population growth must inevitably lead to a situation at which the respective growth rates coincide. At this point the volume of savings is just sufficient to maintain the newly discovered capital–labour ratio. Similar reasoning applies to the opposite situation should $\dot{r}<0$. Thus ultimately $\dot{r}$ approaches zero and the capital–labour ratio remains constant. With a constant amount of capital per capita, the production function then determines the level of income per capita. If income per capita is thus rendered a constant, it follows that the growth rate of the economy as a whole must be exactly in line with the growth rate of population. It is in this sense that we may say that, in the neo-classical model, the rate of growth is determined uniquely by the growth rate of population. Thus, no matter what rate of population growth we may initially assume, the required adjustment in the savings ratio will occur providing a time path of capital accumulation consistent with the maintenance of full employment.

Figure VI.1.

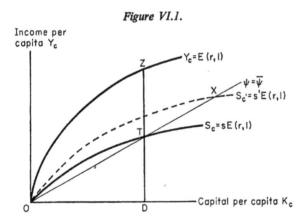

The essence of the argument may be summarized diagrammatically (8). In Figure VI.1, income per capita is measured along the vertical axis and capital per capita along the horizontal. The production function, summarized by the term $E(r, 1)$ then denotes the path of income per capita as a function of capital per capita. Since we are assuming that the production function is linear homogeneous, it

---

(8) The presentation here follows that of H. G. Johnson, 'The Neo-Classical One-Sector Growth Model: A Geometric Exposition and Extension to a Monetary Economy', *Economica*, August 1966.

passes through the origin; it is positively inclined but at a diminishing rate owing to the operation of diminishing returns. Thus

$$\frac{d}{dK_c}(E,1) > 0 \quad \text{and} \quad \frac{d^2}{dK_c^2}(E,1) < 0$$

Since we are assuming that the savings ratio is a constant, the savings function, $sE(r, 1)$ which denotes the amount of saving per capita as a function of income per capita will be a replica of the production function. The vertical distance between the production function and the savings function measures the amount of consumption per capita as a positive function of capital per capita. Finally, since population growth is exogenously determined, its constant growth rate ψ is indicated by the slope of the population function $\psi = \bar{\psi}$.

In Figure VI.1 equilibrium is found at T where the rate of savings growth is just equal to the growth rate of population. The capital–labour ratio is thus maintained as a constant equal to OD. With this amount of capital per capita, the production function determines income per capita equal to DZ. Consumption per capita is represented by ZT and saving per capita by DT. The capital–output ratio is simply DT:DZ. Since all these magnitudes are constants and expressed in per capita terms, the economy in the aggregate must be growing in accordance with the growth of population ψ. It may be noted that no other solution offers a stable equilibrium. At levels of capital per capita in excess of OD, for example, the rate of population growth exceeds the rate of capital accumulation and the capital–labour ratio cannot be maintained. It must fall back towards OD. Likewise, should the initial position imply a capital–labour ratio less than OD the growth of the capital stock exceeds the growth of population. Profit maximizing behaviour and flexibility in comparative factor prices will lead to a raising of the capital–labour ratio towards OD. The position OD, therefore, corresponds to the convergence of r towards zero.

IV. THE SCOPE FOR FISCAL POLICY

If we accept the implications of the model—and it should be emphasized that the model followed here is a highly simplified one-sector, one-commodity model of the growth process—does any function remain for fiscal policy? At first glance the answer is unmistakably no. Taxation may be used to modify the savings function so that $S = I = sY(1-t_y)$ where t_y is the effective average rate of income tax. If the government utilizes the proceeds for direct investment then our savings function becomes

$$S = I = sY(1-t_y)+t_yY.$$

Alternatively, the government may use part of the proceeds in consumption expenditure and part in investment activities whence the savings equation is given by

$$S = I = sY(1-t_y)+pt_yY$$

where p is the percentage of government revenues which are of a capacity-creating character. Hence the introduction of a government sector may either increase or decrease the total volume of savings for any given income-level according to the value of p. However, such a complication can easily be accommodated by making the corresponding adjustment in s. If we denote s' to represent the savings ratio after tax and expenditure changes, then conceptually the equation $\dot{r} = s'E(r, 1)-\psi r$ provides us with a similar solution as before. Although the equilibrium capital–labour ratio will be altered $\dot{r}$ will again converge on zero. The capital–labour ratio will again be a constant, implying a constant per capita income, and the growth of the economy will again be equated with the growth rate of population. Since this is exogenously determined, and presumably unaffected by fiscal policy, the government's tax and expenditure measures have no impact upon the long-term rate of growth.

Diagrammatically, this situation is portrayed in Figure VI.1. We assume that government fiscal policy has been responsible for a raising of the savings ratio indicated by the broken curve, $S_c' = s'E(r, 1)$. The equilibrium position will be shifted to position X, implying a higher capital–labour ratio which in turn implies a higher per-capita income, but the aggregate expansion of the economy continues to be ψ once the new equilibrium has been attained. The inescapable conclusion appears to be that fiscal policy is powerless to influence the overall growth rate.

Even if we were to accept this conclusion—and the reader may be warned that we have no intention of so doing—it does not necessarily imply that fiscal policy has no role to play. Indeed, the role of fiscal policy may well be vital. For, even though fiscal measures may leave the growth rate unaffected, they will certainly influence the volume of consumption. In the recent emphasis upon economic growth and the desirability or otherwise of raising growth rates, it seems to have been forgotten that one fundamental aim of economic endeavour is consumption. Enhanced growth is desirable only to the extent that it permits greater consumption at some future date—and only then if the future consumption streams have been adequately discounted. It should be noted that we are not even concerned with raising income per capita as such, except in so far as it permits greater consumption. It is consumption, and not income which is the index of economic well-being (9). It follows that if the growth rate of the economy is determined solely by population growth, then the government may utilize fiscal policy to influence the savings ratio in the direction of maximum consumption.

Our problem then reduces to a simple one in constrained maximization. Since consumption per capita is simply

$$C_c = Y_c - S_c = E(r,1) - sE(r,1)$$

we wish to maximize this subject to the constraint that

$$sE(r,1) - \psi r = 0.$$

The constraint ensures that we satisfy the stability condition that $\dot{r} = 0$. The economic meaning of satisfying this condition may be interpreted as follows. Fiscal policy measures can be varied so as to select that capital–labour ratio which maximizes consumption per capita as long as the volume of saving then forthcoming is just sufficient to equip the expanding labour force with an identical amount of capital.

We form the function,

$$\Pi = E(r,1) - sE(r,1) + \lambda(sE(r,1) - \psi r)$$

where λ is the undetermined Lagrange multiplier. Setting the partials to zero with respect to r, s, and λ, solving the resulting equations

---

(9) Although, of course, savings may be viewed as a consumption good which enters into the individual's utility function.

provides us with the necessary conditions for maximizing consumption:

$$\Pi_r = \frac{\partial}{\partial r}[E(r,1)] - \frac{\partial}{\partial r}[sE(r,1)] + \lambda\frac{\partial}{\partial r}[sE(r,1) - \psi r] = 0$$

$$\Pi_s = \frac{\partial}{\partial s}[-sE(r,1)] + \lambda\frac{\partial}{\partial s}[sE(r,1) - \psi r] = 0$$

$$\Pi_\lambda = \frac{\partial}{\partial \lambda}[sE(r,1) - \psi r] = 0.$$

In Figure VI.2, the condition for maximizing consumption is attained at position X where the slope of the production function equals the slope of the population function so that

$$\frac{d}{dK_c}[(E(r,1))] = \frac{d}{dK_c}(\psi) \quad \text{and} \quad \frac{d^2}{dK_c^2}[(E(r,1))] - \frac{d^2(\psi)}{dK_c^2} < 0$$

It follows that, if the initial equilibrium position was T, then fiscal policy should be employed not merely to diminish the savings ratio

Figure VI.2

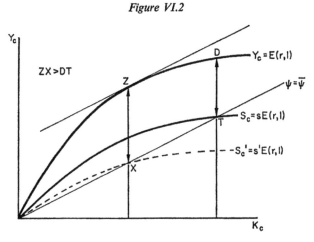

but also to decrease the level of income per capita! Moreover, within the confines of the present model it should be noted that this conclusion is quite independent of the time horizon of the community's indifference curve. Consideration of future generations in no way modifies the policy conclusion that the existing degree of capital accumulation exceeds that which is optimal. Clearly fiscal policy has a major role to play even if we concede that growth rates are exogenously determined.

Other considerations present themselves. Let us assume that an autonomous shift in the saving propensity occurs so as to raise the proportion saved out of any given level of income. According to the model, a new equilibrium will be found at a higher capital–labour ratio. But this conclusion implies a behavioural assumption upon the part of entrepreneurs. The tacit assumption must be that the increase in capital formation lowers the cost of capital investment and induces more capital intensive modes of production. A Keynesian floor to interest rates or interest-inelastic investment demand functions will prevent the required adjustment being made. The situation corresponds to the Harrod–Domar case where the labour force is expanding less rapidly than the required growth of income to maintain full employment of the capital stock. Excess capacity is the outcome. In the neo-classical formulation with the more conventional assumption of Cobb–Douglas production functions, this situation is prevented by increases in the capital–labour ratio. But, as we have already suggested, such an adjustment may be prevented; hence the need for fiscal changes to provide the incentive to adopt more capital intensive methods.

Even if the adjustment process does take place of its own accord, the time interval required may be such as to invite fiscal intervention. Recent theoretical work upon this point has suggested that fiscal policy can appreciably shorten the adjustment period (10). If this be the case, then it follows that active compensatory policy may indeed be essential to ensure that the 'golden age solution' is attained within a time period deemed acceptable by policy-making bodies.

Thus far we have explicitly accepted the neo-classical contention

---

(10) The reference here is to an unpublished manuscript by Douglas Dosser, 'Adjustment through Fiscal Policy in Neo-Classical Growth Models'. The starting point for this discussion will be found in R. Sato, 'Fiscal Policy in a Neo-Classical Growth Model: An Analysis of Time Required for Equilibrating Adjustment', *Review of Economic Studies*, February 1963, and K. Sato, 'On the Adjustment Time in Neo-Classical Growth Models', *Review of Economic Studies*, July 1966.

that the growth rate is determined uniquely by the rate of population growth. It is now time to challenge this underlying postulate. The element which has been ignored is that of technological change. The model hitherto presented has assumed implicitly that technological progress is zero. If technological change is allowed to enter the analysis, as realistically it should, then the rate of population growth ceases to be the sole determinant of growth. If technological progress responds to fiscal incentives, then fiscal policy becomes a joint determinant of the growth process.

Now, there is a considerable body of opinion which leans towards the viewpoint that technological change is embodied within the act of investment. Increasing the rate of investment thus hastens the pace of technological advance. If this is the case—and it should be emphasized that this issue is still a controversial one (11)—fiscal policy which raises the savings–investment ratio is also the vehicle of technical change. Technical progress is revealed in the parametric upward shift of the production function raising the level of per capita income associated with any given capital–labour ratio. It follows, given the assumption of a constant saving propensity, that it also occasions a similar parametric upward shift of the savings function which in turn will generate a new equilibrium corresponding to a higher capital–labour ratio. But, in the process, the attempt to equip each member of the labour force with a larger volume of capital equipment may generate new technological change and the cycle is reinforced. Indeed, there is no reason to assume that stable equilibria will ever be regained, for the impact of technological progress may always counter diminishing returns so as to generate increased savings at a higher rate than population growth. This type of situation is portrayed in Figure VI.3. Again we assume an initial equilibria at T and consider the impact of fiscal policy to raise the savings ratio. In the absence of technological change the new equilibria would be indicated at X—fiscal policy would have attained

---

(11) The rationale for believing that net investment incorporates technical progress is the empirically observed fact that investment activity is seldom mere replacement investment. Usually, the newly acquired capital asset is considered superior to the one which it replaces—witness the remarkable progress in computers, for example. The difficult empirical question, however, fundamental to policy, is whether technical change is an increasing or diminishing function of the rate of investment.

a once-and-for-all change in per capita income without influencing the growth rate. Now, however, we assume that the new investment needed to raise the capital–labour ratio incorporates a degree of technical progress. Both the production function and the savings function are shifted upwards—as indicated by the broken curves— and a new equilibrium is again indicated at Z. But Z need never be attained. Investment induced technology may again occur and the upward shift of the production function is made continuous. In this case the economy is moving along a long-term growth path such as GS with per capita income continually rising. The growth rate of the economy always exceeds that of population growth ψ.

Figure VI.3

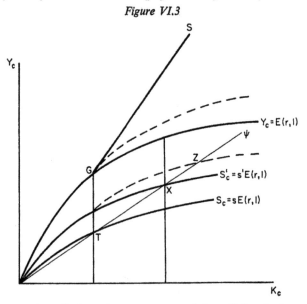

The present analysis, where a once-and-for-all fiscal change takes the economy to the point where technological innovation becomes self-sustaining, is clearly related to the Rostovian economics of the take-off. At low levels of capital per worker, technological progress is inhibited; a certain capital intensity is required before innovation can occur. The task of fiscal policy is to force an increase in savings to transform existing methods of production and attain the required capital intensity. The difficulty faced by so many less-developed countries is how to pursue such a policy when faced with surplus labour resources and the consequent need to adopt labour-intensive methods for full employment.

The foregoing has indicated the importance of introducing technological progress into the neo-classical growth model. Policy measures to induce investment are again of significance in the growth process if such investment embodies technological progress. In recent years the belief that investment is the key to advanced economic growth has led to a series of policy proposals designed to stimulate investment by the private sector. One of these proposals which has received wide endorsement—the so-called strict fiscal–easy money policy for economic growth—will be critically examined in a later chapter in the present work. For the moment, however, it is sufficient to note that we can relate policy proposals directly to the conceptual framework of growth theory. If this is not the case—if policies for economic growth are completely divorced from theoretical considerations—then either the theory or the policy, or both, must be held deficient.

Before concluding the present chapter it is illuminating to apply the present model to an issue of particular importance to the less advanced economies, namely that of population growth. Our theoretical framework has adopted the simplifying assumption that population growth is exogenously determined and expanding at a constant rate ψ. In terms of a developed industrial economy, such an assumption appears perfectly tenable. Below a certain level of per capita income, however, population growth may be more properly regarded as a function of per capita income. Below subsistence income population growth will, by definition, be negative. As income per capita rises above subsistence it is reasonable to assume that population growth responds rapidly as death rates fall. Once death rates have stabilized, the rate of population growth is likely to decline to a more 'normal' level and then become relatively insensitive to further income growth. A variable population growth raises many issues which are portrayed in Figure VI.4 (12). In the

(12) Other complexities can be introduced by making the savings propensity also variable with income per capita. In the present analysis this complication is ignored. It may be noted that *a priori* the impact upon the savings propensity is by no means clear. On the one hand the savings ratio might be expected to increase with rising income. A corollary of the model, however, is that rising income per capita is accompanied by higher capital–labour ratios and hence

H

diagram, no less than three possible intersections occur between the savings and population functions. Of these, points A and C may be regarded as stable equilibria in the sense that any small disturbance will be self-correcting as $\dot{r}$ approaches zero. In contrast, equilibrium at B is unstable and any minor disturbance is perpetuated. If the economy is initially at position A, it is caught in an unenviable low level trap with low per-capita income and consumption. Piecemeal attempts to raise the investment ratio will be self-defeating; the economy will return to A. What is required is a major fiscal effort, possibly accompanied by international aid, to raise capital per capita beyond the level indicated by B. If this is attained the economy will

Figure VI.4

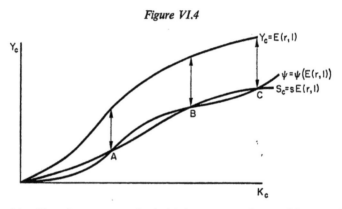

propel itself to the comparatively high consumption and income level C. The argument may be reinforced if we assume position B to denote the capital–labour ratio at which investment induced technological change becomes self-sustaining.

The reader need hardly be reminded that the models employed in the present chapter are extremely simplified. As a basis for practical policy discussion they can provide no more than an elementary conceptual framework pertinent to the issues of growth economics. Nonetheless, it is clear that fiscal parameters have their place in such models—and not least in the neo-classical construct.

---

a lower comparative return to capital accumulation. Logically interest rates should fall.

Chapter VII

STABILIZATION POLICY IN A DYNAMIC SETTING

I. INTRODUCTION

Hitherto, in examining the various policy measures to achieve stabilization goals we have expressly ignored the element of time; or rather we have implicitly assumed the time period required for adjustment to be instantaneous. As an expositional device, such an assumption has the great virtue of simplifying macroeconomic relationships; the desired values of policy objectives are held constant and the actual values adjusted to them simply by the application of policy instruments. Since the adjustment period is infinitely small, neither desired nor actual values may change of their own accord; the advantage of comparative static methodology is that the system is insulated against extraneous shocks. Our attention may be focused solely upon the declared objective and the policy tools at our disposal, and the complexities of changing variables in the real world ignored.

Whilst pedagogically justified, in the realm of practical decision-making such a procedure is clearly faced with difficulties. Apart from the logical inconsistency inherent in assuming a time period so short that nothing can alter—save for those variables we wish to change (1) —for policy purposes the time period of adjustment may be of vital importance. Indeed the choice between using one policy instrument as compared with another may depend upon the time interval required. As we have already indicated, the selection of available policy tools involves a comparative cost–benefit evaluation in which

---

(1) Assuming the time period to be instantaneous is tantamount to making all flow-variables zero. The inconsistency lies in the fact that policy measures themselves incorporate changes in flow magnitudes.

the time element is but one of the factors to be taken into account. In the present chapter, we wish to show the importance of the time element for stabilization policy. Our basic conclusion is that, once time periods are assumed finite, stabilization policy is rendered much more difficult and may even work in a perverse manner—a result of considerable importance to the issue of discretionary versus automatic stabilization policy.

II. A SIMPLIFIED VIEW OF DYNAMICS OF FISCAL POLICY

Before proceeding with the formal analysis, a simple example may serve to outline the essence of the argument. Let us assume that both the desired and actual levels of GNP are a function of time—the former being equated with the desired growth of income compatible with full employment and the latter being a cyclical movement around the long-term desired trend. When the actual level of GNP exceeds the desired level, an inflationary situation is indicated, and when the actual falls short of the desired level, resources are unemployed. Conventional fiscal and monetary policy would indicate a restrictive policy in the former case and expansionary measures in the latter, in order to equate actual and desired income levels. Suppose, however, that a time interval must elapse before the intended policy measures can take effect; in this case it is possible for restrictive monetary and fiscal policy to exert its influence when the economy has already moved into recession of its own accord, or conversely it is possible for expansionary policies to exert their impact when the normal cyclical movements of income are already culminating in an inflationary boom. In this case, illustrated in Figure VII.1 below, stabilization policy serves as a positive destabilizer magnifying the normal movements of the trade cycle.

It remains to enquire as to the reasons for the delayed impact of discretionary fiscal and monetary policy. First of all, time is required before the policy maker can be certain that corrective action is needed. Data are seldom current: a three-month lag in the availability of statistics is often the best that can be expected. Time is also required for analysis; indices of economic activity frequently offer conflicting evidence and underlying trends may be obscured by seasonal influences. Thus, by the time the policy maker is convinced of the need to intervene to correct destabilizing movement of income, such a movement may have already reversed itself. Secondly, major changes in discretionary policy may require legislative approval which may not be readily forthcoming, and the subsequent public debate may contain announcement effects which of themselves exert destabilizing influences. Finally, there is the time needed for proposed measures to take effect which will depend in part upon the differing response patterns of the taxpayer and the banking public.

Figure VII.1

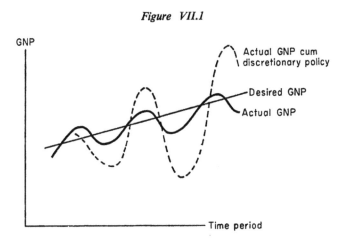

It is this delayed impact of discretionary stabilization measures—which as we have seen may imply perverse destabilizing conse-quences—which has led to the call for the abandonment of attempts at discretionary policy in favour of reliance on purely automatic instruments. The great advantage of automatic stabilizers, it is claimed, is that no time is needed to ascertain the actual position of the economy or to obtain legislative sanction. All that is required is the time needed for actual changes to take effect. Provided that the automatic stabilizers work through instruments with reasonably immediate effects, as, for example, progressive income taxation deducted at source, or unemployment benefits, destabilizing move-ments will not be induced in consequence. Thus, it is argued, the objective should be to dispense with discretionary measures and attempt to improve the automatic stabilizers already included within the monetary–fiscal framework.

Whilst persuasively argued, the case for reliance solely upon automatic stabilizers is difficult to defend. On the one hand, it has long been recognized that automatic stabilizers cannot fully offset a destabilizing income change arising from some autonomous disturbance (2). On the other, as we have previously pointed out in the introductory chapters of this volume, automatic stabilizers cut both ways. They may weaken the force of destabilizing movements within the economy, but they also weaken the stabilizing forces towards recovery when income levels depart from their desired values. The most serious charge against automatic stabilizers, however, is that they too may be destabilizing when viewed in a dynamic setting. Recent theoretical work on this point has developed along two distinct lines. One argument has shown that automatic stabilizers may overshoot their mark when integrated into a simple growth model with progressive taxation (3). The other argues that a suitably lagged consumption function combined with multiplier–accelerator analysis can result in greater instability for the economy with built-in flexibility than without (4). Having indicated the essential points of

---

(2) R. A. Musgrave and M. H. Miller, 'Built-in Flexibility', *American Economic Review*, March 1948.
(3) A. T. Peacock, 'Built-in Flexibility and Economic Growth', in *Stabile Preise in Wachsendar Wirtschaft*, ed. Bombach, Tübingen, 1960.
(4) D. J. Smyth, 'Can "Automatic Stabilizers" be Destabilizing?', *Public Finance*, 1963.

It is necessary to distinguish between the extent of built-in flexibility and automatic stabilization. The two are not synonymous, although they are often treated as such. The degree of built-in flexibility of a tax system measures the responsiveness of tax receipts to a change in income; if tax revenue fluctuates positively with income then it is possible to talk of the built-in flexibility of the fiscal system as opposed to the case where tax revenues are autonomously determined. The question of automatic stabilization, however, refers to the stabilizing consequence of the fiscal system and involves examining the size of the multiplier. Normally, one can show that the greater the degree of built-in flexibility also the greater the extent of the stabilizing consequence—i.e. the greater the degree of automatic stabilization incorporated within the system. This need not always be the case, however, as has been demonstrated by Smyth where built-in flexibility is shown to exacerbate the degree of instability. Smyth's article, it will be noted, really involves a misnomer. To the question 'Can automatic stabilizers be destabilizing?' the answer must be unmistakably no, by definition. A more accurate title—although lacking the same dramatic impact—would have been 'Can built-in flexibility be destabilizing?' to which, as Smyth has demonstrated, an affirmative answer is possible.

what is admittedly a difficult branch of fiscal policy, we turn now to a more formal analysis.

III. A SHORT-TERM DYNAMIC MODEL

Let us adopt a simple national-income model which combines the accelerator principle with the Keynesian multiplier (5). Assuming a closed economy, national income at time n is given by

$$Y_n \equiv C_n + I_n + G_n$$

Consumption we assume to be a linear function of income in the previous period and we simplify the analysis by assuming average and marginal propensities to be equal; i.e. we dispense with consumption at zero income. Accordingly we have

$$C_n = bY_{n-1}$$

Investment we assume to be geared to changes in consumer demand. A simple version of the accelerator concept makes investment depend upon the change in consumption over the previous period. Thus we may write

$$I_n = \Omega(C_n - C_{n-1})$$

or alternatively

$$I_n = b\Omega Y_{n-1} - b\Omega Y_{n-2}$$

Finally, we assume that at some stage in the past the government launched an expenditure programme, let us say for defence, and has maintained its defensive commitment at a constant level ever since. Thus

$$G_n = G_{n-1} = G_{n-2} = \ldots G_{n-n} = \bar{G}$$

The level of national income is now given by

$$Y_n = b(1+\Omega)Y_{n-1} - b\Omega Y_{n-2} + \bar{G}. \qquad . \qquad \text{(VII.1)}$$

That is to say, the level of national income for any period is uniquely determined by a non-homogeneous second-order difference equation

---

(5) The model presented here follows Paul A. Samuelson's classic article 'Interactions between the Multiplier Analysis and the Principle of Acceleration', *Review of Economic Statistics*, May 1939.

with constant coefficients. Its solution is a comparatively straight-forward exercise given by the equation

$$Y_n = k_1 x_1{}^n + k_2 x_2{}^n + \frac{-d}{a+b+c} \qquad . \qquad . \quad \text{(VII.2)}$$

where $a = 1$
  $b = -b(1+\Omega)$
  $c = b\Omega$
  $d = -G$

and x_1 and x_2 are the solution to the quadratic equation, $ax^2 + bx + c = 0$, obtained in the usual way (6), and where k_1 and k_2 are found by comparing two given initial conditions, or income levels (7). The equation is non-homogeneous owing to the constant level of government expenditures. In the absence of taxation, this constancy of government spending implies that we are dealing with a model of income determination which has no discretionary stabilizing element. These assumptions are sufficient to generate a time sequence of income change whose character is determined solely by the values we assign to the multiplier and accelerator coefficients. There are four possible cases to consider. At one extreme a zero or low value of the accelerator may be sufficiently dwarfed by the multiplier so that the initial expenditure by the government sector leads to a raising of the income level to a new equilibrium which is then maintained as a constant. This is in accordance with the simple Keynesian case where investment is assumed exogenous. At the opposite extreme, a high value of the accelerator is sufficient to generate an explosive move-ment of income which rises without limit (8). For our purpose it is the intermediate cases which are of greater interest. Depending upon the values we select for the multiplier and the accelerator we may generate a continual cyclical movement of income which displays either damped or increasingly instable fluctuations. These cases are

---

(6) i.e. $x = \dfrac{-b \pm \sqrt{b^2 - 4ac}}{2a}$

(7) A useful introduction to the solution of difference equations which deals specifically with the Samuelson model is given by W. J. Baumol in his *Economic Dynamics*, second edition, pp. 151 ff.

(8) It is this case which forms the basis of the Hicksian theory of the trade cycle. Cf. J. Hicks, *A Contribution to the Theory of the Trade Cycle*, 1950.

illustrated in Figure VII.2 together with the intermediate borderline case where the opposing influences are just exactly offset culminating in a cyclical movement of constant magnitude.

The foregoing has assumed the absence of discretionary stabilization policy. Let us now modify the analysis by assuming that the government expenditure programme is designed to act in a counter-cyclical manner. Our purpose is to show that discretionary changes by the government sector may heighten the degree of instability already inherent within the system.

Figure VII.2

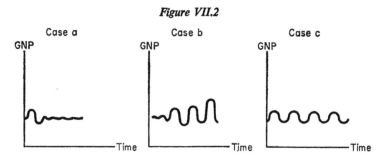

Again let us assume that the government maintains its defence expenditure at a constant level, irrespective of the income level. In addition, however, we now assume that, following the initial period in which the defence programme was established, additional outlays are incurred or cut back in the attempt to stabilize the economy. Suppose that the government is aiming at a 'target' level of income Y^* compatible with full employment. If income in the previous period falls short of the target level, additional outlays are incurred in the current period; if income in the previous period exceeds the target level, expenditures are reduced. Thus we assume that the government reacts to income changes with a one-period lag just as consumers do, but in the opposite direction. In this case our government expenditures function may be written

$$G_n = G_d + \mu(Y_{n-1} - Y^*)$$

where G_d represents the constant defence expenditure and μ is the stabilization coefficient. μ is of course negative; we may also assume that μ is less than unity. The government, having mastered the intricacies of multiplier analysis in the initial part of this volume will adjust μ to its estimate of the marginal propensity to save. It will not attempt to make up any short fall in the desired level of income entirely by itself. Such a policy would clearly overshoot the mark and be destabilizing but this is obviously a trivial case. Rather, μ will be increased when b falls and vice versa. Thus our assumptions postulate no more than rational sophisticated behaviour upon the part of the government desirous of stabilizing the income level at Y^*. What are the consequences?

To answer this question let us refer to the rather special Case c illustrated in Figure VII.2. Here it is assumed that the values of the multiplier and accelerator coefficients are just sufficient—with government expenditures held constant—to generate continuous regular fluctuations in income which neither die out nor become explosive, but are maintained at a given magnitude. Superimposed upon this model, the modified expenditures equation is sufficient to generate increased cyclical instability without necessarily changing the character of the income sequence. The cycles continue indefinitely as before but are now of a more violent and unstable nature as a consequence of compensatory expenditure changes.

A numerical example may serve to clarify the argument. Let us assume that the marginal propensity to consume is equal to 0·5, implying a multiplier of 2, and the accelerator coefficient is 2. If defence expenditures are maintained at a level of 1 (billion) then, in the absence of compensatory expenditures changes, the income sequence will be as shown in section A of Table VII.1. This example is one provided by Samuelson in his initial article (9). Consider now the compensatory expenditures function with the stabilization coefficient −0·5. This implies that the government taking the size of the multiplier into account attempts to rectify any divergence from the target level of income by an expenditure change of 50 per cent of the discrepancy in the reverse direction. We also assume that the target income level is 3 (billion). The results are summarized in section B of Table VII.1.

Thus not only does the adoption of countercyclical expenditures policy increase the magnitude of fluctuation between peak and trough, but the cyclical movement itself is speeded up. Compensatory

_____

(9) In the original article the income level for period seven is incorrectly given as ·9141.

policy serves to increase the frequency of the trade cycle. The comparative positions are summarized in Figure VII.3.

There is, however, one redeeming feature of compensatory policy. The total income generated for the periods calculated is significantly

Table VII.1

	A		B	
$Y_n = b(1+\Omega)Y_{n-1} - b\Omega Y_{n-2} + 1$			$Y_t = b(1+\Omega)Y_{n-1} - b\Omega Y_{n-2} +$ $+ 1 + \mu(Y_{n-1} - Y^*)$	
$b = 0{\cdot}5\ \Omega = 2$			$b = 0{\cdot}5\ \Omega = 2\ \mu = -0{\cdot}5\ Y^* = 3$	
Period	Y_n	G_n	Y_t	G_n
1	1·0	1·0	1·0	1·0
2	2·5	1·0	3·5	2·0
3	3·75	1·0	5·0	0·75
4	4·125	1·0	4·0	0·00
5	3·4375	1·0	1·5	0·50
6	2·0313	1·0	0·0	1·75
7	0·6094	1·0	1·0	2·50
8	−0·1172	1·0	3·5	2·00
9	0·2148	1·0	5·0	0·75
10	1·4395	1·0	4·0	0·0
11	2·9443	1·0	1·5	0·5
12	3·9771	1·0	0·0	1·75
13	4·0212	1·0	1·0	2·50
14	3·0548	1·0	3·5	2·0
15	1·5610	1·0	5·0	0·75
16	0·2867	1·0	4·0	0·0
17	−0·1310	1·0	1·5	0·5
18	0·5169	1·0	0·0	1·75
19	1·9063	1·0	1·0	2·50
20	3·3427	1·0	3·5	2·00
21	4·1076	1·0	5·0	0·75
22	3·8188	1·0	4·0	0·0
.	.	.	.	.
.	.	.	.	.
.	.	.	.	.

greater in the case of compensatory action than without. This arises because the compensatory action is designed to secure an income level in excess of the average of the non-compensating income sequence. Thus arises a delicate issue of 'trade-off'. Increased instability may be the price that society pays for higher overall per capita income and growth. Despite the mechanistic nature of the present example such a consideration is undoubtedly of significance to the issue of discretionary versus automatic stabilization.

It remains to enquire into the cause of this destabilizing impact. The answer is comparatively simple and can be given without delving into the mathematics of difference equations. It stems from the fact that by adopting a target level of income the government is behaving

Figure VII.3. Fluctuations in Y_n with and without compensatory expenditures.

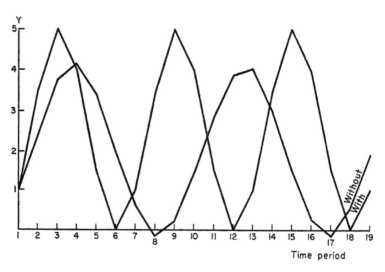

in what is an essentially arbitrary and random manner. If income in the period $n-1$ exceeds the target level, the government cuts back upon its planned level of expenditures *irrespective* of the response of investment in the private sector. Clearly, as long as the investment sector is concerned solely with the change in the volume of consumer demand, this decrease in government spending may coincide with expansionary or contractionary movements as the case may be. Our policy measure may be compared to the percussion player who strikes the timpani every time the conductor looks in his direction. On occasions it may help the performance along; more often it will not.

IV. AUTOMATIC STABILIZATION IN A DYNAMIC SETTING

(a) The short-term case

If the case against countercyclical policy is that it may intensify cyclical movements what is the case for automatic stabilization? It is a simple matter to take account of built-in flexibility merely by adopting a proportional income tax. In this case our consumption function becomes

$$C_n = b(1-t_y) Y_{n-1}$$

where t_y is the tax rate which is assumed invariant through time. The net effect of the income tax is to reduce the size of the marginal propensity to consume. In our example considered above, the introduction of the tax is clearly a stabilizing device; it is easily shown, for example, that the introduction of a 50 per cent income tax is more than sufficient to turn our continuous oscillation Case c into an ultimately stabilizing movement as represented by Case a.

However, as Smyth has demonstrated (10) it is dangerous to generalize from such simple models. Substituting a slightly more complex consumption function into our analytical framework so that consumption is made a function of disposable income of the previous two periods, it is possible for built-in flexibility to exert a perverse effect. Thus, if

$$C_n = b_1 (1-t_y) Y_{n-1} + b_2 (1-t_y) Y_{n-2}$$

where

$$(0 < b_1 < 1, \quad 0 < b_2 < 1, \quad 0 < b_1 + b_2 < 1)$$

then under certain conditions (11) the presence of built-in flexibility, as indicated by the proportional income tax, will increase the extent of instability. Moreover, in certain cases, it is possible for the existence of built-in flexibility to turn a damped oscillatory movement of income as in Case a of Figure VII.2, into an increasingly unstable situation as indicated in Case b.

(b) The long-run case

Thus far, we have dealt with the question of built-in flexibility, and

---

(10) Smyth, D. J., 'Can "Automatic Stabilizers" be Destabilizing?', op. cit.
(11) I.e. if the roots of the characteristic equation are complex.

the resultant degree of automatic stabilization in a short-term setting. In this case, built-in flexibility is assumed to exist when tax receipts vary directly and positively with income changes. In contrast, built-in flexibility would be absent in the case where tax revenues were autonomously determined and independent of the income level. When we turn to a simple-growth model, however, the question must be raised as to whether or not such a definition is appropriate. If, in a growing economy, income is expanding constantly over time we would naturally expect a similar expansion of fiscal revenue without considering this in any way to be an indication of built-in flexibility (12). For positive built-in flexibility to exist within a growth context, we shall require that the fiscal system behaves in a progressive fashion, that is to say that the tax revenue grows more than proportionately to income. Conversely, we shall assume that the absence of built-in flexibility is indicated by fiscal receipts remaining a constant propor-tion of national income.

Having defined built-in flexibility of the fiscal system in this manner, a modified Harrod–Domar model is sufficient to demon-strate our basic point, namely that in an expanding economy the presence of built-in flexibility may be too potent and may cause the system to overshoot the equilibrium growth path of income. The model presented here differs slightly from the formulation adopted in Chapter VI (13). There, it was sufficient to demonstrate that taxes and government expenditures could influence the long-term growth path of income necessary for full employment of the capital stock. For that purpose a simple Domar formulation with autonomous invest-ment spending was quite sufficient; there was no need to involve ourselves with the intricacies of difference equations. Now, however, a more complex policy problem requires more complex tools of analysis; again we will invoke second order difference equations (14).

Following our analysis of Chapter VI, let us again assume that the

---

(12) To consider an extreme example, in a growing economy even a window tax would generate additional revenues over time; one would hesitate to cite this as an example of built-in flexibility of the fiscal system, however.

(13) The model presented here is in fact taken from A. T. Peacock, 'Built-in Flexibility and Economic Growth', in *Stabile Preise in Wachsender Wirt-schaft*, ed., Gottfried Bombach, Tübingen, 1960.

(14) To which, we were assured, there is no general solution, the equations being non-linear. For this reason we will again utilize numerical examples.

increase in capacity income in any period n, is a simple function of investment in the previous period, irrespective of whether the investment is undertaken by the private or the public sector. Thus again we may write

$$\Delta Y_n^c = \sigma(I_{n-1} + pG_{n-1})$$

where σ is again the output–capital ratio and p is that percentage of government expenditure assumed to be of a capacity creating character. Let us also assume, however, that investment by the private sector is itself a function of the income level of the same period. Thus

$$I_n = \Omega Y_n$$

where Ω is an accelerator coefficient for the private sector. Let us further assume that the proportion of government expenditure upon investment activities, p, remains a constant, and that total government expenditure is also a constant function of the level of national income. In this case, we may write

$$G_n = g Y_n \quad \text{and} \quad pG_n = pg Y_n$$

It follows that the total of resources channelled into investment activities, whether by the private or the public sector, in any period n, is simply $\Omega Y_n + pg Y_n = \rho_n$ where ρ is a constant proportion of national income. Accordingly, the increase in capacity income is simply given by

$$\Delta Y_n = \sigma \rho$$

Turning to the demand side of the economy, national income in money terms is given, as before, by the conventional identity

$$Y_n^m \equiv C_n^m + I_n^m + G_n^m$$

Now, however, let us assume that consumption is a lagged function of disposable income of the previous period. In this case we have

$$C_n^m = b Y_{n-1}^m (1 - t_y)$$

where t_y is the average rate of tax and is assumed to be constant, i.e. that there is no built-in flexibility in the sense defined above. Investment by the private sector we know to be a constant function of income in the same period, and likewise government expenditure is also given as a constant proportion of national income. Thus,

$$I_n^m = \Omega Y_n^m$$
$$G_n^m = g Y_n^m$$

The level of money national income at period n therefore is obtained by simply solving the linear difference equation so that

$$Y_n^m = \left[\frac{b(1-t)}{1-(\rho+g)} \right]^n Y_0^m$$

which may be written

$$\frac{\Delta Y^m}{Y} = \frac{b(1-t)}{1-(\rho+g)} - 1$$

Equilibrium growth thus requires the increase in monetary national income to equal the increase in capacity output so that:

$$\left[\frac{c(1-t)}{1-(\rho+g)} \right] = (\sigma\rho+1)$$

The following numerical example illustrates the equilibrium growth path, assuming arbitrary values of the coefficients:

Table VII.2: Equilibrium Growth
$(b = \cdot9, t = \cdot1, g = \cdot1, \rho = \cdot15, \sigma = \cdot53)$

Periods	Y^r	Y^m	C^m	G^m	T^m	S^m Govt. $(T^m - G^m)$	S^m Private $Y^m - (C^m + T^m)$	I^m	Price index
1	1000	= 1000	750	100	100	—	150	150	100
2	1080	= 1080	750	108	108	—	162	162	100
3	1166	= 1166	875	117	117	—	174	174	100
4	1259	= 1259	944	126	126	—	189	189	100
.	.	.	.	.	.	.	.	.	.
.	.	.	.	.	.	.	.	.	.
.	.	.	.	.	.	.	.	.	.

The example illustrates the case where the economy moves along the equilibrium path, growth requirements being fulfilled without inflation. Following established convention, we associate changes in the price index with the divergence of the paths of equilibrium growth and actual growth of national income, so that the price index is given by the following formula:

$$P = \frac{1+(\Delta Y^m/Y^m)}{1+(\Delta Y^r/Y^r)} \cdot 100$$

In our 'equilibrium' example the price index displays no movement in view of this convention.

Clearly, if there is an upward change in the coefficients b or g, i.e. a rise in the rate of consumer or government expenditure, then, with no change in the tax coefficient, the actual growth of money income will exceed the equilibrium growth and the general price level will rise at an increasing rate. In the case of a rise in the investment coefficient, the general result does not differ, but the inflationary movement is partially offset by the effect of the real rise in the rate of investment on the equilibrium rate of growth. In other words, in a 'no flexibility' situation as defined for the growth case, an inflationary movement caused by an increase in one or more of the spending coefficients will not be offset by the rise in tax receipts.

We now consider the effects of two autonomous changes which have the same initial impact on the level of national income. We shall first of all assume an upward change in the investment co-efficient, ρ, and secondly an upward change by the same amount in the government expenditure coefficient, g.

The only other change we allow is in the tax system. It is now assumed that a progressive rate structure obtains, so that a rise in income produces a more than proportionate rise in tax revenue and thus a rise in the average rate of tax. In short, the value of the tax coefficient depends on the rate of change of income which can be represented in the following formula (15):

$$t_{yn} = t_{yn-1} + \mu(Y_{n-1} - Y_{n-2})$$

---

(15) It must be admitted straight away that a two-period lag in adjustment of the rate structure is adopted for analytical convenience. It is quite realistic to assume that tax liabilities are not lagged while tax assessments and pay-ments are, but it is a moot point whether taxpayers' consumption is a function of income after actual tax deducted or after allowing for tax liabilities, i.e. whether taxpayers think in 'cash' or 'accrual' terms. It is assumed here that they think in cash terms—like the authors.

I

Change in the investment coefficient, ρ

Using the above equations and assuming a rise in ρ, the system will be disequilibrated. The rise in investment will increase the rate of income generation, producing an initial inflationary effect. However, this effect will be gradually offset by two forces. The first is the effect of the rise in the rate of net investment on the real rate of growth. The second is the rise in the value of the tax coefficient, t_y, caused by the process of income generation itself. At some point in time, the path of growth tendencies will cross the path of the equilibrium growth of income. This must be so because, with all coefficients constant with the exception of t_y, which rises as national income rises, money national income will grow, but at a decreasing rate, while the

Table VII.3: Built-in Flexibility and Growth; Case I
$(b = \cdot9; t_1 = \cdot1; \mu = \cdot0003; g = \cdot1; \rho = \cdot2; \sigma = \cdot53)$

Period	Y^r	Y^m	C^m	G^m	T^m	S^m Govt.	S^m Private	I^m	P
1	1000	= 1000	750	100	100	—	150	150	100
2	1080	< 1157	810	116	116	—	231	231	107
3	1194	< 1269	888	127	187	60	194	254	106·3
4	1321	< 1336	936	134	241	107	161	267	101·1
5	1461	> 1373	961	137	275	138	137	275	93·9
⋅	⋅	⋅	⋅	⋅	⋅	⋅	⋅	⋅	⋅
⋅	⋅	⋅	⋅	⋅	⋅	⋅	⋅	⋅	⋅
⋅	⋅	⋅	⋅	⋅	⋅	⋅	⋅	⋅	⋅

equilibrium rate of increase will remain constant, i.e. equilibrium national income will rise exponentially. At some point, therefore, the built-in flexibility of the tax system will make the system 'overshoot' the mark as the path of actual income generation crosses the equilibrium growth path. This situation contrasts with that found in the macro-static case, where with a progressive tax system it is not even possible to re-establish the full employment level of national income at a predetermined price level. The point at which the paths of actual income and equilibrium income will cross will depend on the extent of the change in ρ, the value of μ and the lag in tax assessment.

A second numerical example (Table VII.3) will perhaps clarify these results, which spring essentially from the fact that, with a progressive tax structure, the process of growth generates increases in fiscal receipts in excess of the growth of public expenditures. The induced deflationary impact increases with the passage of time; ultimately it becomes sufficient to 'over-stabilize' the economy and force a level of national income below the equilibrium level.

This phenomenon, that of a continuous raising of the fiscal surplus, has received wide attention in recent years, especially in the United States where it has been termed the 'fiscal drag' and linked with another important concept, that of the full employment budget

Figure VII.4

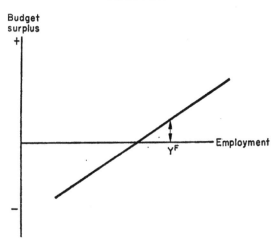

surplus (16). The latter may be defined simply as the potential budget surplus which would obtain at a full employment level of income, given existing expenditure patterns and tax rates. Diagrammatically, we can convey the essence of the argument in Figure VII.4. Here it is assumed that the fiscal surplus is a direct function of employment level, assuming expenditure policies and tax rates remain unchanged. At full employment a small budget surplus is attained. At less than full employment the surplus is speedily eliminated and a deficit results as expenditure is increased (unemployment benefits, welfare

(16) See *Economic Report of the President*, Washington, 1962.

payments, etc.) and as tax revenues fall. Conversely, as the income level exceeds the full employment level, implying inflationary conditions, a larger fiscal surplus is automatically generated due both to the normal expansion of fiscal receipts and the cut back in government relief and assistance payments. The slope of the function, therefore, indicates the degree of built-in flexibility of the budget system (17).

Whereas the slope of the function provides a measure of the built-in flexibility of the budget, a parametric shift of the function would imply a discretionary fiscal change, either on the tax side, expenditure side or both. So far, our discussion of the full-employment budget surplus has been static in nature in that we have taken a snapshot of the function at a given point in time. Now, however, let us allow for dynamic changes. If, as we have indicated, economic expansion is accompanied by an expansion of fiscal receipts in excess of increased expenditure, then over time the fiscal surplus will be increased for any given employment level (18). The budget function will shift gradually upwards as revenue expansion outpaces expenditure growth. This is the nature of the 'fiscal drag' which is thus tantamount to a discretionary restrictionary fiscal change. The concern was voiced in the late 1950s and early 1960s that this continued tendency would exert a progressively deflationary impact upon the economy and slow the rate of economic growth. If the nature of fiscal drag is akin to restrictive discretionary measures then is not the remedy immediately apparent, namely that of a phased decrease in the rate of tax over time?

But this is precisely the solution to our problem of over-stabilization of the fiscal system when tax rates are progressive. The problem of fiscal drag and problem of excessive automatic stabilization are

---

(17) It is important to note, however, that it does not in any way indicate the degree of automatic stabilization incorporated into the budget system. This is because the multiplier impact of an expenditure change will—according to the balanced budget theorem—normally differ from that of a tax change. Consequently, it is quite possible for a decrease in the extent of the fiscal surplus to exert a deflationary impact upon the overall economy if attained by the combined workings of a tax and expenditure decrease where the fall in revenues exceeded the decline in expenditures. The concept of the full employment budget surplus, therefore, should be used with caution when considered as an index of the degree of automatic stabilization.

(18) The full employment level being, of course, defined in percentage terms.

essentially one and the same; they both spring from the desire of modern societies to incorporate a degree of progressivity within the fiscal system. As long as this remains the case, the solution must lie in the ability and willingness to adopt discretionary policies, to offset the undesirable consequence of combining progressivity and economic growth (19).

To argue that automatic stabilizers are inadequate, or involve undesirable consequences necessitating compensatory action, does not resolve entirely the choice between discretionary fiscal changes and reliance upon automatic weapons. The question of degree remains; to what extent should discretionary changes be invoked; even if automatic stabilizers cannot be ever fully adequate should we still not try to make the system as automatically stabilizing as possible? Unfortunately there appears to be no simple answer to these questions. On the one hand, a value judgement is involved as to how far should discretionary action be permitted to interfere with the normal functioning of the market economy. On the other, the political feasibility of enacting discretionary fiscal changes may be vital in determining the outcome. In the United Kingdom, the comparative ease and speed of obtaining legislative approval would tend to support the case for discretionary changes. In contrast, in the United States, the comparative difficulty of obtaining legislative sanction, and the great uncertainty surrounding the timing of policy changes, would tend to reinforce the arguments for reliance upon automatic stabilizers and perhaps also for greater dependence upon monetary policy (20). For our purposes, it is sufficient to note that logical difficulties confront either policy, and when considered in a dynamic setting such difficulties are generally enhanced.

---

(19) Although this conclusion may be questioned; see in particular, Vito Tanzi 'A Proposal for a Dynamically Self-Adjusting Personal Income Tax', *Public Finance*, No. 4, 1966, for an interesting alternative solution. What Tanzi's approach really amounts to is a variant of formula flexibility which fundamentally is no different in principle from reliance on built-in flexibility.

(20) Not requiring the approval of Congress.

Appendix to Part I

A SIMPLE NON-LINEAR MODEL OF FISCAL POLICY

I. INTRODUCTION

Most of our models have been constructed with linear functions. One could argue that the parameters in the equations would, in practice, be capable of estimation, and that there is no need to assume that throughout the time period in which the values of aggregates are being observed the values of the parameters need remain constant. However, once it is agreed that non-linear functions would better represent our hypotheses about firms' and households' behaviour, it becomes rather tedious to keep changing the values of the fixed parameters throughout the process of adjustment from one initial equilibrium position to another. Building on previous elementary mathematical techniques, it is a relatively simple matter to generalize the models used and, in particular to remove the restriction of linearity.

Another characteristic of our models is that the specification of the parameters in the equations results in a proliferation of symbols. Once it is recognized that a particular variable depends on more than one independent variable, e.g. consumption being a function of both income and the rate of interest, very complicated expressions emerge, a good example being equation II.6. A generalized model which concentrates on functional relationships rather than the exact nature of the underlying equations, e.g. $i = i(Y, MS)$ rather than $i = (vY + \gamma - MS)/c$, gets round this difficulty. Alternatively, for roughly the same 'input' of symbols, we can examine more complicated and possibly more realistic hypotheses.

In what follows, we shall build a non-linear system which includes some of the main features of previous models, but with no disaggregation of the kind found in Chapter IV. The mathematical techniques used are total differentiation and matrix multiplication, which have already been employed separately in previous analysis.

II. A SIMPLE NON-LINEAR MODEL

We shall first of all employ a simple model, very similar to the one used in Chapter V, for an open economy, with a government sector and which includes a monetary equation as well as income equation.

$$Y = C+I+G+X-M$$
$$C = C[Y(1-t_y)-\eta]$$
$$I = I(i)$$
$$M = M(Y)$$
$$i = i(Y, MS)$$

G, X and MS are autonomous variables and are defined as before

M = imports
C = private consumption
t_y = proportional income tax rate
η = taxes invariant with income, and also autonomous
i = bond rate of interest

It will be noted that the various expressions above are put in functional form. The exact nature of the equations are not specified. For example, $I = I(i)$ means that Investment is a function of the rate of interest, but we do not specify the exact nature of the function as we did previously in making it a linear function of the rate of interest.

On examination, we find that we can reduce these functional relationships to three equations with three unknowns I, M and i and with three fiscal policy variables, G, T and t_y.

Thus

$$Y = C[Y(1-t_y)-\bar\eta]+I(i)+\bar G+\bar X-\bar M$$
$$M = M(Y)$$
$$i = i(Y, \overline{MS})$$

Taking the total derivatives of each equation and re-arranging terms, we obtain the following:

$$\left\{ \begin{array}{l} dY[1-(1-t_y)C_y]+dM-I_i di = dG+dX-C_y d\eta \\ -M_y dY \qquad\qquad +dM \qquad = 0 \\ i_y dY \qquad\qquad\qquad di = i_{MS}dMS \end{array} \right\} \quad (A.1)$$

which may be written as

$$
\begin{bmatrix}
C^X & 1 & -I_i \\
-M_y & 1 & 0 \\
-i_y & 0 & 1
\end{bmatrix}
\begin{bmatrix}
dY \\
dM \\
di
\end{bmatrix}
=
\begin{bmatrix}
dG+dX-C_y d\eta \\
0 \\
i_{MS} dMS
\end{bmatrix}
\tag{A.2}
$$

where $C^X = 1-(1-t)\,C_y$.

(The subscripts denote partial derivative, so that, for example,

$$
M_y \, dY = \frac{\partial M}{\partial y} \cdot dY)
$$

Inverting the matrix we obtain:

$$
\begin{bmatrix}
dY \\
dM \\
di
\end{bmatrix}
= \frac{1}{\Delta}
\begin{bmatrix}
1 & -1 & I_i \\
M_y & C^X - I_i i_y & I_i M_y \\
i_y & -i_y & C^X + M_y
\end{bmatrix}
\begin{bmatrix}
dG+dX-Cd\eta \\
0 \\
i_{MS} dMS
\end{bmatrix}
\tag{A.3}
$$

where $\Delta = \det. A = C^X + M_y - i_y\,Ii$.

In explaining the working of the model, we shall confine attention to the *direction of change* (+ or −) in the dependent variables (Y, M, i) resulting from a change in the value of the independent policy variables (G, T and M).

First of all, we determine the signs of the partial derivatives as follows:

$$
0 < C_y, M_y, < 1; \quad I_i, i_{MS} < 0; \quad i_y > 0
$$

In addition, $0 < t_y < 1$.

With this information, we find, first of all, that det. $A = \Delta$ is positive. Further, we can now re-write adj. A, substituting the signs for the partial derivatives. For example, if we take the element a_{32}, this is $+I_i(My)$. $I_i < 0$, $My > 0$ so that the whole term is negative $[(+)(−)(+)]$.

$$
\begin{bmatrix}
dY \\
dM \\
di
\end{bmatrix}
= \frac{1}{\Delta}
\begin{bmatrix}
+ & - & - \\
+ & + & - \\
+ & - & +
\end{bmatrix}
\begin{bmatrix}
dG+dX-C_y d\eta \\
0 \\
i_{MS} dMS
\end{bmatrix}
$$

Multiplying through in the usual manner, and listing our policy variables vertically and dependent variables horizontally, we can

observe how the former change the value of the latter. We can add
to our list of dependent variables the balance of payments change
defined as $dB = dX - dM$. The direction of change will simply be
determined by dM, with $dX = 0$. Similarly we can add to our list
of independent variables the balanced budget change $dG + d\eta$ where
$dG = d\eta$:

Dependent Variables →		dY	dM	di	dB
I n d e p e n d e n t	V a r i a b l e s				
		dG +	+	+	−
		$d\eta$ −	−	−	+
		dMS +	+	−	−
		$dG+d\eta$ +	+	+	−

While the direction of change can be determined by the model,
what can we say about the magnitude of change? With MS exogenously determined, the model does not specify the nature of the
monetary effects of any budgetary change. Consequently, if we
change G, for example, any consequential effects on monetary
supply which would affect the rate of interest, and, in turn, investment and income, are not recorded in the model. Nevertheless, we
can reach the familiar conclusions about the effects of *equal* changes
in G and η and also in the balanced budget. This is because, for
example, if we compare an increase in G with an equal decrease in η
and assume that the resultant initial deficit is financed by increases
in cash, the expansion in money supply will be identical. Similarly,
in the balanced budget case the initial change in the deficit/surplus
is zero. There is therefore no reinforcing effect offered by changes in
money supply.

Therefore, using expression A.3

$$\frac{dY}{dG}=\frac{1}{\Delta},\ \frac{dY}{d\eta}=-C_y.\frac{1}{\Delta},\ \frac{dY}{(dG+d\eta)}=(1-C_y).\frac{1}{\Delta}$$

Clearly, £ for £, an increase in government expenditure increases Y by a greater amount than a reduction in taxation of equal amount, the change in cash deficit being identical. Increasing G would have a greater multiplier effect than a balanced budget change of equal amount, but an interesting curiosity is revealed by the fact that this result only follows for an equal decrease in η, if $C_y>\cdot5$!, given our model. This last comparison, however, stresses the need to consider monetary effects, for the tax change increases the supply of cash in the system, but the balanced budget does not.

III. FURTHER ANALYSIS

Having mastered the simple mathematical techniques displayed above and their application to fiscal policy models, the reader should try his hand at following some of the professional literature which has increasingly adopted the method of formulation explained in Section II above. Useful examples are

D. J. and A. F. Ott, 'Monetary and Fiscal Policy: Goals and Choice of Instruments', *Quarterly Journal of Economics*, Vol. LXXXII, 1968;

R. N. Cooper, 'Macroeconomic Policy Adjustment in Interdependent Economies', *Quarterly Journal of Economics*, Vol. LXXXIII, 1969.

Both these articles also cover the subject-matter of Chapter VIII of this volume.

PART TWO

FISCAL POLICY AND THE THEORY
OF ECONOMIC POLICY

Chapter VIII

POLICY TARGETS AND FISCAL INSTRUMENTS

I. INTRODUCTION

Thus far, our primary concern has been to outline the theory of fiscal policy, essentially in a Keynesian context, and focusing attention upon fluctuations in the aggregate level of output. On occasions we have utilized our output variable as a proxy for employment and prices; by extending the analysis to the external sector we have also dealt specifically with issues arising from balance of payments considerations. Throughout, however, in outlining the basic theory our conceptual framework has been essentially uni-dimensional. We have dealt with a single-valued objective function. Whilst changing the objective at will in order to extend the scope of our analysis we have nonetheless treated each objective in isolation. Although eminently suited to the process of model building it must be conceded that such a procedure drastically simplifies the problem of economic decision-making when applied to the real world.

The first step in attaining greater realism in economic policy making is to recognize that both objectives and instruments are multi-dimensional. This entails specifying precisely both the goals to enter into the objective function and the policy tools available for their attainment. Two approaches are then possible: on the one hand we may assume that the policy objectives once specified are immutable; the question then reduces to combining sufficient policy instruments to realize their achievement. This we may refer to as the Hansen/Tinbergen approach to economic policy and it will be illustrated in the present chapter. A second approach we may refer to as the optimizing approach illustrated in the work of Theil. This discusses specifically the extent to which all or any of the policy goals may be modified in the event of conflict in order to maximize the welfare of society. An example which has become popular in recent years is afforded by the Phillips curve. Here it is assumed that both full employment of the labour force and avoidance of inflation are desirable goals which however are in conflict. A 'trade-off' is involved in that a higher level of employment entails a greater pace of inflation and vice versa. The optimizing approach attempts to determine the extent to which both goals are to be compromised in order to maximize economic welfare given the preferences of society. In In contrast, the Hansen/Tinbergen approach implies the search for new policy instruments (for example an incomes policy) by which both objectives may be achieved simultaneously. The following chapter will take up examples of the pragmatic approach of trade-off; for the present we will assume that policy objectives are immutable and we seek the policy tools for their attainment. The fundamental conclusion of the Hansen/Tinbergen analysis is that given a specific number of policy targets an equal number of policy instruments is required for their realization.

II. OBJECTIVE FUNCTION

For purposes of illustration let us assume that there are only two policy goals pertinent to the objective function, namely full employment and balance of payments equilibrium (1).

Accordingly, our objective function may be expressed as

$$u = u(x, y)$$

where u represents the ordinal utility index which we are trying to maximize and x and y are the respective policy goals. We assume that there are values of x and y which will maximize the welfare of the decision maker. These values, which we assume correspond to full employment income and balance of payments equilibria, we denote by $\bar{x}$ and $\bar{y}$. Thus,

$$u(\bar{x}, \bar{y}) > \begin{matrix} u(\bar{x}, y) \\ u(x, y) \\ u(x, \bar{y}) \end{matrix}$$

---

(1) Cf. the wellknown article by R. A. Mundell, 'The Appropriate Use of Monetary and Fiscal Policy for Internal and External Stability', *IMFSP*, March 1962.

Insisting upon the immutability of our policy objectives implies that
no other values except $\bar{x}$ and $\bar{y}$ are admissible from the decision-
maker's standpoint. It follows that, as long as $\bar{x}$ and $\bar{y}$ are attained
simultaneously, the choice of policy instruments is irrelevant. Any
combination of instruments remains as good as any other providing
the utility function is maximized.

III. THE MODEL

In all but the most trivial cases it is assumed that both objectives
will respond to more than one policy instrument. This is the nature
of interdependence which implies that no one policy tool may be
uniquely related to any given target or objective. For present

Figure VIII.1

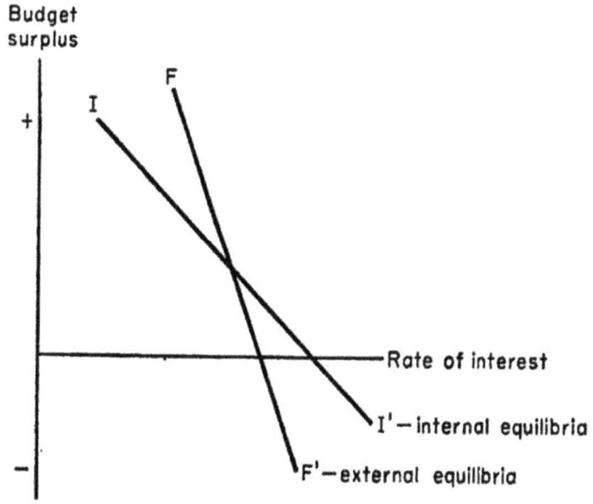

purposes let us assume that both objectives respond to fiscal policy—
defined here to mean variations in the size of the budget surplus—as
well as to monetary policy denoted by changes in the level of interest
rates. The essence of the argument may then be conveniently
summarized in terms of Mundell's original diagram.

In Figure VIII.1, we measure the budget surplus, positive or
negative upon the vertical axis and the rate of interest upon the
horizontal. Let us now consider all possible combinations of budget
surplus and rate of interest consistent with the maintenance of full

employment without inflation. Clearly, the locus of such a function will be negatively sloped since it is assumed that the deflationary impact of higher interest rates must be offset by an increase in spending if aggregate output is to be maintained. Similarly, consideration of all possible combinations consistent with balance of payments equilibria will reveal a negatively sloped function since any decrease in the budget surplus will worsen the balance of trade (2), and require a compensating improvement upon the capital account through higher interest rates. Let us now consider the slopes of the respective functions. The external function will possess the steeper slope. This follows from the fact that the balance of trade (exports minus imports) will be constant throughout the range of the employment function since both are a function of income. If capital is sensitive to interest rate movements, then a movement down the internal function implies a continual improvement upon the external account. In order to maintain equilibrium, therefore, a smaller interest-rate change will be needed to compensate any variation in the budget surplus in the case of the balance of payments function than in the case of the employment function. Thus the external function will possess the steeper slope and will intersect the internal function at a unique point which reconciles both internal and external policy requirements. Thus the appropriate use of two policy instruments enables us to achieve both targets of our objective function simultaneously. Let us now modify the analysis slightly by taking into consideration the issue of economic growth (3). A popular policy proposal advocated in recent years argues that monetary and fiscal policy may be combined in order to raise growth rates. The essence of the proposal involves the transfer of resources from consumption to investment. Stated briefly, this is to be achieved by a strict fiscal policy designed to curtail existing consumption combined with an easy monetary policy and retirement of the debt to induce investment of the proceeds. Providing the correct mix of monetary and fiscal policy is pursued, virtually any rate of growth

---

(2) Since any expansion of income leads to an increase of imports in excess of any induced expansion of exports. Cf. pp. 50–57.
(3) The following draws heavily upon a paper by one of the authors, G. K. Shaw, 'Monetary-Fiscal Policy for Growth and the Balance of Payments Constraint', *Economica*, May 1967.

is considered attainable. The immediate appeal of such a policy lies in the fact that the attainment of successively higher growth rates is perfectly consistent with the maintenance of full employment; for, whilst increased taxes necessarily imply reduced consumer expenditures, the level of aggregate demand is maintained by the offsetting increase in investment activity. Accordingly, there need be no conflict between the goals of full employment and enhanced growth. The correct monetary–fiscal mix is designed to achieve both. Basically the essence of the proposal may be reduced to one simple proposition: for any given level of budget surplus or deficit there will be but one specific rate of growth, providing the rate of interest is low enough to ensure investment of the available funds.

If we attempt to combine this analysis with the preceding argument, however, it follows at once that whatever combination of budget surplus and interest rate reconciles the internal and external equilibria conditions must also determine the growth rate. Once the equilibria conditions have been established, any attempt to raise the overall growth rate must be at the expense of internal or external stability—or indeed of both. And in view of the political impossibility of departing from the two stability conditions for any prolonged period of time, the growth rate ceases to be a policy variable; it becomes exogenously imposed upon the system. The pursuit of three interdependent objectives with only two policy instruments is logically impossible. One of the objectives must either be sacrificed or, as in the case of the growth rate, passively determined.

More formally, our objective function is now represented by the function

$$u = u(x, y, z)$$

Where z is the growth objective. But as long as the permissible values for x and y are already determined so that $x = \bar{x}$ and $y = \bar{y}$, z is determined as a residual.

The argument is summarized in Figure VIII.2 where the rectangular areas denote the permissible growth rate applicable to any combination of interest rate and budget surplus. Thus a balanced budget is consistent with a 3 per cent growth rate, provided the rate of interest is 4 per cent. Equally, a £300 million fiscal surplus will allow a rate of growth of 6 per cent, assuming a rate of interest of 1 per cent.

K

Assume an initial situation at point C. This satisfies both internal and external equilibrium conditions of the Mundellian model with a £100 million fiscal surplus and a 3 per cent interest rate. But such a combination also ensures a 4 per cent growth rate. Moreover, any attempt to increase the overall growth rate requires both higher taxes and lower interest rates. An additional £100 million in tax receipts together with a reduction of the interest rate to 2 per cent is needed to raise the growth rate by one percentage point—a movement from C to D. A raising of the growth rate is of course perfectly consistent with the maintenance of full employment. Indeed, since policy

Figure VIII.2

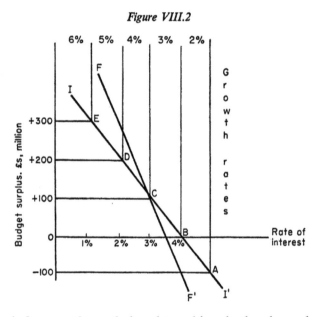

proposals for growth are designed to achieve both enhanced growth and full employment without inflation, the locus of points A to E, while tracing out what we may term the 'growth opportunity curve', are also coincident with the Mundellian internal stability function. It follows at once that adoption of a policy for a higher growth rate involves a deficit upon the external account. Further, equilibrium in the balance of payments can only be regained either by accepting substantial unemployment—which is assumed to be ruled out politically—or by discontinuing the growth policy and raising interest rates. Thus in the last analysis the stability conditions, both internal and external, determine the rate of growth.

Thus far, we have expressly followed Mundell in assuming that the budget surplus is an index of fiscal control. This, however, is to overlook the fact that a budget surplus can be increased in two ways; by increasing tax yields with expenditures held constant or alternatively by decreasing expenditures with tax revenues unchanged. Conventionally, as we have previously indicated, a government

Figure VIII.3

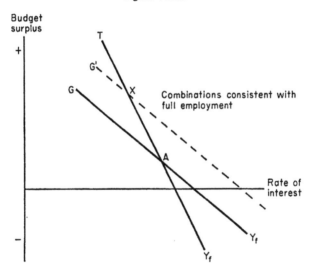

expenditure increase will be more high-powered than an equivalent decrease in taxation. Consequently, for any given increase in budget surplus, it will require a larger offsetting variation in interest rates in the case of a decrease in expenditures than it will in the case of higher taxes. What this amounts to is that the function describing the locus of budget surplus-interest rate combinations consistent with the maintenance of full employment will be steeper in the case of a tax change than in the case of an expenditure change. This situation is portrayed in Figure VIII.3.

The diagram assumes an initial full employment equilibrium at point A, where the two functions coincide. Any movement along one of the functions implies a new equilibrium being attained where the functions will again intersect at a new combination of interest rate and budget surplus. Thus, if a combined tax increase and interest rate decrease leads to a new equilibrium at X, we immediately form a new internal function using G′ as the expenditure function.

The introduction of the balanced budget multiplier principle modifies the pessimism of our original findings by permitting an element of choice over the permissible growth rate. For now there is more than one budget surplus/interest rate combination consistent with the maintenance of both internal and external equilibria. The analysis may be completed by reference to Figure VIII.4.

Figure VIII.4

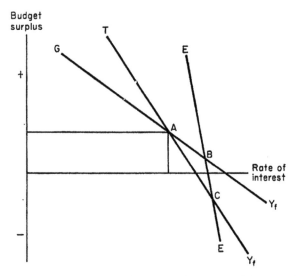

In this case we assume an initial situation at position A. Although this is consistent with the maintenance of full employment it also implies a deficit upon the external account. Both full employment equilibria and balance of payments equilibria can be achieved by either increasing government expenditures and raising interest rates in moving to B or alternatively by decreasing taxes and raising interest rates as implied by position C (or, of course, by some combination of the two). From the growth viewpoint, position B will be preferred; the higher budget surplus and lower interest rate will be more conducive to investment.

The reader will appreciate that the discretionary power attained in the sphere of growth policy is a direct consequence of implicitly introducing another policy instrument—namely the size of the government sector for any given budget level. Economic growth becomes a policy variable because the number of instruments is brought into equality with the number of objectives.

The initial situation portrayed in Figure VIII.4 assumes full employment income, combined with a balance of payments deficit. As we have seen, the optimal solution in terms of enhanced growth implies an increase in government spending as opposed to a decrease in taxation. Thus attainment of the optimal growth path would necessitate an increase in the ratio of public to private goods. This is most probably the situation in most countries with external deficits as, for example, the U.K. prior to the devaluation of 1967. There is, however, nothing inevitable in this outcome. Had the external function interested the internal function to the left of point A, then the initial situation would have corresponded to full employment income and a payments surplus. Full equilibria would then have required an increased rate of taxation as opposed to a decrease in public spending, if the maximum permissible growth rate is to be attained. Since the tax proceeds are to be transferred to the private sector, no change would occur in the ratio of public to private goods. Thus one surprising conclusion of the analysis is that a payments deficit indicates the possible need to raise the public/private goods ratio, whilst a payments surplus has no such implication but merely suggests a change in the consumption/investment ratio in the private sector.

Whilst the additional policy instrument permits an area of discretion in determining the growth rate, it nonetheless remains true that an upper limit is imposed by the need to maintain both internal and external equilibria. Mathematically, we can express this as a simple problem in constrained maximization. In the present model the growth rate may be considered as a simple function of investment by the private sector plus government spending where the latter is of a capacity creating character. Thus we may write

$$Y^g = \sigma(I + pG)$$

where Y^g symbolizes the growth rate of income and p is the proportion of government expenditures which are essentially in the nature of investment. The essence of the Mundellian analysis is that both employment and balance of payments equilibria may be considered a function of the budget surplus and interest rates. Thus

$$Y^F = Y^F(D, i)$$
$$B = B(D, i)$$

where D denotes the budget surplus and B the balance of payments surplus. Expressing the budget surplus in terms of expenditures and taxes—which permits us to take account of the modification introduced by the balanced budget multiplier—we have

$$Y^F = Y^F(G, T, i)$$
$$B = B(G, T, i)$$

where T is the tax yield. If full employment prevails initially it is still possible to vary G, T, and i whilst respecting the employment objective as long as the following condition is respected.

$$dY = \frac{\partial Y}{\partial G} dG + \frac{\partial Y}{\partial T} dT + \frac{\partial Y}{\partial i} di = 0$$

This we may refer to as the full employment constraint which traces out the boundaries of the internal stability function. Likewise, given initial balance of payments equilibria, variations in G, T, and i are permissible as long as the total differential is maintained at zero. Thus

$$dB = \frac{\partial B}{\partial G} dG + \frac{\partial B}{\partial T} dT + \frac{\partial B}{\partial i} di = 0$$

summarizes the balance of payments constraint, and traces out the external stability function. The permissible growth rate is then derived from the function:

$$\Pi = \sigma(I + \rho G) - \lambda_1 \left(\frac{\partial Y}{\partial G} dG + \frac{\partial Y}{\partial T} dT + \frac{\partial Y}{\partial i} di \right)$$
$$- \lambda_2 \left(\frac{\partial B}{\partial G} dG + \frac{\partial B}{\partial T} dT + \frac{\partial B}{\partial i} di \right)$$

where λ_1 and λ_2 are the undetermined Lagrange multipliers.

That the growth rate should be constrained arises from the fact that the third policy instrument is not a truly independent one. The size of the public sector is variable only within the limits of the budget surplus applicable to full employment income and balance of payments equilibria once the level of the budget has been determined. Given the inflexible nature of the full employment and balance of payments objectives, the permissible growth rate is again determined as a residual. Freeing the growth rate from this constraint would require a further policy tool as, for example, exchange rate flexibility, investment incentives, technological change and the like.

Nonetheless, the present analysis is useful in illustrating the nature of the maximization problem when one or more policy objectives is accorded priority. The constraint upon the permissible rate of growth disappears once employment levels and balance of payments surpluses are permitted to be variable. A social welfare function, possibly encompassing the preferences of generations yet unborn, might well allow a measure of unemployment in the interests of higher growth. This naturally leads us into the difficult question of trade-off, where no one objective is granted priority, *a priori*, over any other. This will be the subject matter of the following chapter.

Chapter IX

FISCAL POLICY AND CONSTRAINED MAXIMIZATION

I. INTRODUCTION

As explained in Chapter I and Chapter VIII fiscal policy is not used in a policy situation in which it would be normal to have only one objective, represented by a single value of one macro-variable. In the policy situation facing governments, there may be several objectives to be met simultaneously, such as internal stability, balance of payments 'equilibrium', and a 'satisfactory' rate of economic growth. Nor is the budget the only instrument which may be used in order to attempt to meet the chosen objectives. Earlier chapters have indicated, at least implicitly, that an 'inactive' monetary policy may frustrate the operation of fiscal policy in achieving only one objective represented by a 'target' value of national income.

In Chapter VIII we saw that an important question is left unanswered if we think of the policy problem as one of achieving simultaneously two targets expressed in terms of single values of two macro-variables. If it is impossible to achieve both these values simultaneously, what is the 'best' policy to adopt? There is no particular reason why the 'next best' to not being able to achieve both values is to seek to achieve one, and to accept *any* value of the other which results from policy action. It may be that a preferred position would be one in which *neither* target value is achieved. Thus achieving a 'target' employment level in which 99 per cent of the working population is employed, might mean, given the nature of the economy and the policy instruments available to influence its structure, accepting a rate of increase in the price level of 4 per cent per annum. At the other extreme, achieving complete price stability so that the rate of increase in the price level is zero, might mean allowing the employment level to fall to, say, 92 per cent. There is good reason to suppose that, faced with these awkward facts of economic life, the community might prefer a lower employment level than the target value, if it meant a rate of increase in the price level lower than 4 per cent per annum. In contemporary jargon, it might be possible to identify the 'trade-off' between employment level and the rate of increase in price level which allows us to delineate a *preference function* for the community.

The analytical method which enables us to examine the problems posed by 'trade-off' between policy objectives may be introduced by considering the familiar example of the optimizing procedure of the individual household. We assume in microeconomic analysis that the household's objective is to maximize utility, subject to an income or expenditure constraint.

Expressed in the usual mathematical form, the utility of individual consumer, A, is a function of the commodities he buys; for simplicity we assume that there are only two commodities, l and m, which are competing substitutes, so that:

$$u^A = u^A(l, m)$$

The consumer attempts to maximize this function subject to an income constraint. Assuming that all income is spent on l and m, and that the prices (P_1 and P_2) of l and m are given, then this constraint may be written:

$$E(l, m) = P_1 l + P_2 m = Y^A$$

The algebraic solution to such equations, which demonstrates how maximization of utility is achieved, need not be reproduced here, as it will be presented later. Readers will be aware that its geometric counterpart is the tangency of the individual's highest indifference curve with the 'budget line' whose slope depends on the price ratio P_1/P_2. All that need be mentioned here is that it is possible to develop the analysis of constrained maximization situations in order to understand the role of fiscal policy in optimizing the welfare of the community, when welfare is no longer associated with only one variable, the level of national income.

It is clearly a big step from the specification of the individual utility function to some form of community indifference system, and from the simple 'budget line' registering the opportunities of the individual to purchase goods l and m to the identification of an analogous constraint on community choice. At the same time, as we hope to demonstrate, understanding the logic of constrained maximization is an important first step in the economist's comprehension of the problems of matching policy aims with the policy instruments which we have already examined. Some of the practical problems in applying the logic are introduced in the final chapter of this volume.

II. EXAMPLE 1: THE EMPLOYMENT/INFLATION TRADE-OFF

In our first example, which is a highly simplified one, two policy objectives of the community are identified and are associated with two economic variables. The first is the price level, or rather its rate of change through time, i.e. $\dot{P} = dP/dn \cdot 1/P$. The objective is to minimize the value of $\dot{P}$, subject, however, to achieving simultaneously a 'satisfactory' level of employment. The second objective, therefore, is to minimize the amount of unemployment, denoted by U. By definition, 'the best of all possible worlds' is reached when the value of both $\dot{P}$ and U are zero, which would be represented by the origin in a two-dimensional diagram with $\dot{P}$ measured along one axis and U along the other (see Figure IX.1). However, it is assumed that the 'cost' of reducing the value of $\dot{P}$ is a rise in the value of U. Following the conventions of welfare theory, we can draw a series of community indifference curves which delineate the 'trade-off' between the rate of price change and unemployment. We assume that over a specified range of $\dot{P}$ and U the indifference curves are both concave to the origin and also continuous. Thus, the 'trade-off' between $\dot{P}$ and U denotes that successive equal decrements of $\dot{P}$ can only be 'bought' by successive decrements of U of diminishing value. More formally, we describe the community's objective function, π, as

$$\pi = \pi(\dot{P}, U) \qquad . \qquad . \qquad . \qquad \text{(IX.1)}$$

$$\left(\frac{\partial \pi}{\partial \dot{P}}, \frac{\partial \pi}{\partial U} < 0\right)$$

Although it is not fundamental to the analysis, we may introduce two constraints. It would not be too unrealistic to assume that there is a maximum value of $\dot{P}$ which the community will tolerate, whatever the value of U, and, equally, a maximum value of U, whatever the value of $\dot{P}$; e.g. $\dot{P} = 10$ per cent per annum, and $U = 6$ per cent of working population.

The community could reach its chosen nirvana at the origin, but this is not vouchsafed by the operation of the market economy. The 'opportunity slope' of the community is represented by the relationship between the rate of change in the price level and the unemployment rate which results from market forces. In this contribution, we shall conveniently domesticate the Phillips curve for our use, which is based on the observed relationship, in a number of countries, between the two variables. This relationship is represented by a downward sloping curve in a two-dimensional system with $\dot{P}$ on the vertical and U on the horizontal axis as shown by L in Figure IX.1. A common algebraic form of this relationship (1) is

$$\dot{P} = \varepsilon + \zeta U^{-1} \qquad . \qquad . \qquad . \qquad \text{(IX.2)}$$

$$(\varepsilon < 0 \quad \text{and} \quad \zeta > 0)$$

The problem of policy is to minimize $\dot{P}$ and U, subject to the constraint represented by the Phillips curve. The identification of the fulfilment of this condition is easy. It is simply the point of tangency between the Phillips curve and the highest (concave) community indifference curve, denoted by A.

This is a simple example of a constrained maximum problem which can be solved by the usual Lagrange undetermined multiplier technique.

Max.
$$\pi = \pi(\dot{P}, U) \qquad \left(\frac{\partial \pi}{\partial \dot{P}}, \frac{\partial \pi}{\partial U} < 0\right) \qquad . \qquad \text{(IX.3)}$$

Subject to
$$\dot{P} - \varepsilon - \zeta U^{-1} = 0 \qquad (\varepsilon < 0, \zeta > 0) . \qquad . \qquad \text{(IX.4)}$$

Forming the Lagrange function

$$\pi = \pi(\dot{P}, U) + \lambda(\dot{P} - \varepsilon - \zeta U^{-1})$$

---

(1) The reader will recall the discussion in Chapter V of the relation between prices, employment and output, and our emphasis on the special assumptions used in the Keynesian model, which assumes no trade-off between employment and the price level.

and setting its partial derivatives equal to zero, the solution is

$$\lambda = \left(\frac{\partial\pi/\partial U}{\partial\pi/\partial\dot{P}}\right) = \frac{\zeta}{U^2} \qquad . \qquad . \qquad . \qquad (IX.5)$$

where λ is the Lagrange multiplier.

However, this 'best-in-an-imperfect-world' solution is not attained automatically. Given the familiar macroeconomic explanation of the working of a market economy, economic fluctuations would be

Figure IX.1

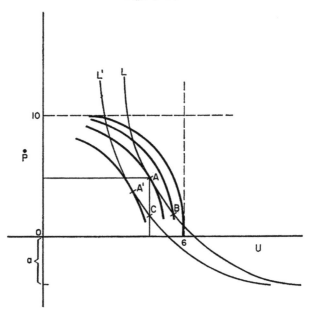

reflected in continuing movement along the 'opportunity slope' so that, in the absence of government intervention, it would be pure chance if the system settled for any length of time at A. Keynesian purists, indeed, would argue that if the system were stuck, say, at B, in underemployment equilibrium there would be no guarantee that intervention in the form of monetary policy would be able to shift the system towards A. Thus the task of fiscal policy is to regulate purchasing power in such a way as to reach A, and *to keep it there*, assuming the community's preference system remains unchanged.

The task of the government economists is to specify the relationship between the change in the budget parameters and the change in the price level and unemployment. The link between the latter, the policy variables, and the former, the policy instruments, is implicit in the analysis in Chapter V. There we show that the link is a strong one, if Keynesian-type assumptions are realistic, i.e. if the marginal product of labour = the average product of labour and the wage rate remains constant up the defined level of full employment of labour. These particular assumptions, as already pointed out (see page 86) assume no trade-off between the level of employment (unemployment) and the price level, if labour is the only variable cost of production. We cannot simply insert equation V.7 in a suitably modified form at this stage in order to establish the link, i.e. an increase in N is equivalent to a fall in U so that

$$\frac{-dU}{dG} = \left[\frac{1}{1-b(1-t_y)} \right] \cdot (\varepsilon) \qquad \text{(IX.6)}$$

We have therefore to take account of the fact that the Phillips curve states that a decrease in U must be associated with an increase in P, so that ε, for example, can no longer be regarded as a constant.

It can be accepted that if the economy is below the acceptable rate of unemployment, then an increase in aggregate demand will produce an increase in output and reduce unemployment but 'at the cost of' some increase in P, as specified by the Phillips curve. Therefore we may write

$$U = U(Q) \qquad \text{where } U_Q < 0$$
$$Q = Q(Y) \qquad \text{where } Q_y > 0$$
$$Y = Y(G, t_y) \qquad \text{where } Y_G > 0, Y_{ty} < 0$$

G = expenditure on goods and services by government.
t_y = 'the' tax rate.

It would follow that the usual conclusions regarding fiscal policy would obtain, but in a modified form. Increasing government expenditure would reduce unemployment and decreasing it would increase unemployment: and vice versa for a change in 'the' tax rate.

One interesting point emerges from this analysis. As we have seen in Chapter V, if we alter the 'mix' of taxes between taxes on income and taxes on consumption, we may get changes in the price level which are independent of those caused by changes in the wage rate or the marginal productivity of labour (cf. equation V.8). Consider a situation in which the initial conditions for optimization were satisfied, but for some policy reason it was decided to maintain the same level of aggregate demand, but with a rise in the rate of consumption taxes balanced by a fall in the rate of income tax. (This is, of course, tantamount to introducing an additional constraint, which might reflect government policy on income distribution.) With no shift in Y, there would be no shift in Q or in U, but the price level would rise with the rise in t_i. There would then be an upward shift in the Phillips curve in Figure IX.1. This is perhaps a healthy reminder that, whatever the origins of the Phillips curve as a statistically observed relationship, we have to treat it as a logical construct in this context. In any case, several writers have cast doubt on the desirability of its 'hold' on the economics profession because of the difficulty in squaring its empirical foundation with several of the influential hypotheses of economic behaviour.

Speculation in recent years has centred in the possibility of shifting the curve to the left, through the use of an appropriate incomes policy. In this context, we assume that this is possible, and can use the opportunity to illustrate once again the problem of co-ordination of fiscal policy with the use of other policy instruments.

A new curve, L', is drawn to the left of the original one, L, which denotes that, for a given fiscal policy, $\dot{P}$ can be held at a lower value for a given level of unemployment. If fiscal policy remains unchanged, the point C is attained which is preferred to A. The interesting point, however, is that this is not the optimal situation for the community would prefer to be at A' rather than C with a lower level of unemployment and a higher $\dot{P}$. The result of the (successful!) operation of an incomes policy means that fiscal parameters must be changed to adjust the system to reach A'. In short, this offers again a useful illustration of Bent Hansen's important point that attainment of given ends presupposes an optimal mix of policies and therefore co-ordination between the various authorities responsible for them.

A word of warning is necessary at this stage of the analysis, and which may bear repeating at a later stage. It is comparatively easy to add to the number of policy instruments which might be brought to bear on the shape and location of the opportunity slope. In any policy situation, however, it would be naive to assume that the choice of policy instruments does not affect the social welfare function. In the above example, an incomes policy may very well achieve a shift in the opportunity slope, as represented by the Phillips curve, but its distributional effects may require us to add another dimension to the social welfare function. Put in another way, the social indifference system may not remain stable throughout the process of adjustment from point A to C to A', in which case it is impossible to say whether or not the new policy 'mix' has improved social welfare.

III. EXAMPLE 2: GROWTH AND CONSUMPTION

Let us assume that the two elements in the social welfare function are growth and consumption defined in the following way:

$dY/dn \cdot 1/Y = y$ where y is the percentage rate of growth in a period of time;

C/Y $= x$ where x is the proportion of national output devoted to consumption.

It is further assumed that the 'trade off' between y and x can be represented by the usual set of indifference curves denoting the declining social utility of growth with respect to consumption. We may also add in two constraints. There is some minimum 'tolerable' percentage of output to be devoted to consumption, e.g. a subsistence minimum, and some minimum 'tolerable' growth rate, perhaps because a growth rate below that level would result in an 'intolerable' level of unemployment given a growing labour force.

We can now write our social welfare functions as

$$\pi = \pi(x, y) \quad \text{where } \pi_x, \pi_y > 0 \qquad . \qquad \text{(IX.7)}$$

The next stage of our analysis is to identify the production relations in the economy which will enable us to determine the 'opportunity line' relating growth and consumption. Clearly, it is reasonable to suppose that a community which sacrifices consumption at the margin can have a higher rate of growth, abstracting from problems associated with maintaining full employment of resources and the terms of trade between the relevant country and its trading partners.

Let us assume that there is no problem about maintaining the level of aggregate demand sufficient to produce full employment of resources and that the economy is a closed one.

One such relation between sacrifice of consumption and increase in growth is implicit in our previous Harrod–Domar growth model, viz. that for a given level of *ex ante* investment (= *ex ante* saving) and ICOR, we can predict the rate of growth of the economy. In order to avoid problems associated with the dependence of output on the growth of the labour force, we can assume that capital and labour are employed in fixed proportions and that, for any values of y and x in the welfare function, there is no labour constraint. We can achieve the optimum rate of growth (as later determined) without ear of labour shortage.

We can now write out simple production function as

$$\frac{dY}{dn}\cdot\frac{1}{Y} = \frac{\dot{Y}}{Y} = y = 1/\phi\cdot\rho \qquad . \qquad . \qquad \text{(IX.8)}$$

where $\phi = \text{ICOR} = 1/\sigma$ and is assumed constant $\phi = \phi$
$\rho = I/Y = $ proportion of investment to GNP

There is no depreciation of capital, so that gross investment = net investment.

If the economy has no problems in reaching the warranted rate of growth path, $I_n/Y_n = S_n/Y_n = 1 - C_n/Y_n$ for all n. It follows that we can write:

$$C/Y = x = (1-\rho) \qquad . \qquad . \qquad . \qquad \text{(IX.9)}$$

and from equation IX.8, as $y\bar{\phi} = \rho$ expression (IX.9) can be re-written as:

$$x = (1-\bar{\phi}y) \qquad . \qquad . \qquad . \qquad \text{(IX.9a)}$$

We now have a social welfare function, which can be maximized, subject to the 'production constraint'

$$\pi = \pi(x, y) \qquad \pi_x, \pi_y > 0$$

subject to

$$x = (1-\bar{\phi}\cdot y)$$

Using the Lagrange multiplier

$$\Pi = \pi(x, y) + \lambda(1 - \bar{\phi}y - x)$$

$$\Pi_x = \pi_x - \lambda = 0 \qquad . \qquad . \qquad . \qquad . \qquad \text{(IX.10a)}$$

$$\Pi_y = \pi_y - \lambda\bar{\phi} = 0 \qquad . \qquad . \qquad . \qquad . \qquad \text{(IX.10b)}$$

$$\Pi_\lambda = (1 - \bar{\phi}y - x) = 0 \qquad . \qquad . \qquad . \qquad \text{(IX.10c)}$$

Substituting in (IX.10a), we have:

$$\pi_x - \frac{\pi_y}{\bar{\phi}} = 0$$

or

$$\frac{\pi_x}{\pi_y} = \frac{1}{\bar{\phi}}$$

As before, we can express our results in graphical form as in Figure IX.2. The indifference curves are given the usual shape, and the slope of the opportunity line LM *must be equal to the value of the ICOR*, for $dx/dy = -\bar{\phi}$. The optimal position is by definition that point where I' touches the opportunity line. Therefore, with $\bar{\phi} = 3$, and the optimal consumption level, i.e. $x = 9/10$ (OA), then solving for y in equation IX.9a gives us a rate of growth of 3·33 per cent per annum (OB).

Although the example used assumes a constant ICOR, this is not a necessary restrictive assumption. Assume a variable ICOR, e.g. ϕ, then we can re-write $x = 1 - f(\phi) \cdot y$ so that $dx/dy = -f(\phi)$. The opportunity line then becomes concave to the origin.

There is no reason to suppose that the economic system would automatically achieve the optimal position, as determined by the shape of the social welfare function, any more than, in our previous example, it would achieve exactly the optimal trade-off between the rate of changes in prices and the unemployment rate. This is not to say that we have any *technical* means of choosing whether or not a 'non-interventionist' situation with, say, a lower rate of growth and higher consumption rate, is any better or worse than another trade-off which requires fiscal intervention. It is sufficient for our purpose

L

to know that governments in practice frequently carry out policies, often in response to popular demand, to intervene.

The policy question is, therefore, how to move the economy along the opportunity line, or possibly to adjust the slope of the line itself, in order to optimize, given the social welfare function. It is conceivable that there may be fiscal policies which could lower the value of ϕ and therefore 'swivel' the line to the right starting from point A.

Figure IX.2

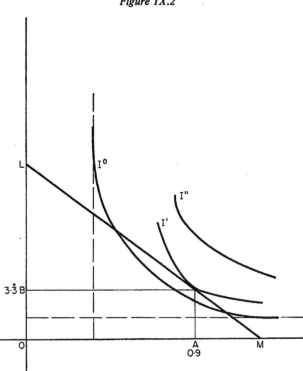

For the moment, let us concentrate on the ways in which the government can alter the investment rate, ρ, by fiscal means, it being the only remaining independent variable in the production function.

Having already assumed that there is no policy problem about maintaining full employment of resources, in the sense that an increase in aggregate saving will not reduce consumption to the level where there will be excess capacity caused by lack of effective demand, we can view the policy task as that of releasing resources for investment purposes by the use of the budget. Raising the level of aggregate saving by fiscal means is an obvious way of obtaining this release of resources, as already explained in Chapter VI, for the government can influence the rate of private and public saving by adjustments in tax rates and government expenditure rates. This can be demonstrated very simply by equating ρ with government saving (the excess of taxes [less transfers] over current expenditure on goods and services) and private saving (the excess of personal income [less taxes] over personal expenditure on current goods and services). We neglect business saving.

$$\text{Then } \rho = I/Y = \frac{sY(1-t_y)}{Y} + \frac{(t_y-g)Y}{Y}$$

where s = proportion of personal income saved, $0<s<1$
t_y = 'the' tax rate—a proportional tax on income, $0<t_y<1$
g = proportion of real national produce devoted
    to government expenditure on current goods
    and services, $0<g<1$

More simply still

$$\rho = \frac{I}{Y} = [s(1-t_y)+(t_y-g)]$$

We obtain the familiar conclusion that, £ for £, lowering the rate of government spending, g, is a more effective means of raising the investment ratio, ρ, than raising the tax rate, t_y. This follows from the proposition that, whereas t_y raises the *ex ante* budget surplus (or reduces the deficit), it also reduces disposable incomes and, by our assumptions, also reduces the level of private savings. The converse is also true.

As in the previous example, the reader must be warned that it is one thing to indicate the way in which the theory of economic policy explains the role of fiscal policy in maximizing some community welfare function, but it is another thing to draw precise conclusions applicable to any particular situation. The point may be illustrated by considering the use of a change in t_y as a means of optimizing the welfare function. On the one hand, a rise in t_y may affect the level of growth not only through its effect on raising the level of saving which 'permits' the higher investment rate which is assumed to be necessary in order to optimize. It is conceivable that it could also lower the growth rate through its effect on the incentives to work. Therefore, the opportunity slope itself may shift as a result of the use of a particular policy instrument. Again, a change in the tax rate which produced changes in the distribution of income, might lead the community, through its representatives, to consider that the welfare function had not been correctly specified, or that a 'distributional constraint' had not been taken into account. Although this warning is needed, it does point to one useful feature of even a simplified exposition of the theory of economic policy, namely the emphasis it lays on having explicit information about the nature of the objective function, and all the relevant information about the constraints which govern the process of maximizing it.

IV. EXAMPLE 3: EMPLOYMENT CREATION IN DEVELOPING ECONOMIES

Our final example of constrained maximization is that of employment creation within the developing economies. This implies a departure from our former analysis in that hitherto, when discussing employment policies, we have explicitly adopted a Keynesian framework. That is to say, we have normally assumed that when resources are unemployed an increase in aggregate monetary demand will stimulate an expansion of physical output and raise the numbers of those engaged in productive employment. The essential assumption underlying Keynesian policies to alleviate unemployment is that supply conditions are elastic. Low levels of output are solely the consequence of a lack of effective demand and raising the level of aggregate demand—either by reducing taxation, raising government expenditures, or extending credit—is indicated as the appropriate remedy.

One of the more interesting questions in present-day economics is whether such a conceptual framework is applicable to the problems confronting the 'developing economies'. Our interest is mainly in those economies with extensive unemployment—either open or disguised—which are often referred to as the surplus labour economies. It is generally conceded that the existence of such unemployment with all the attendent social and political difficulties cannot be tolerated, particularly with regard to the induced inflow of agrarian unemployed to the urban areas.

It is commonly argued that under these conditions Keynesian policies are inapplicable in the attempt to expand employment opportunities. Unemployment is seen as the consequence not of a deficiency of effective demand but rather due to the excess of labour in relation to the available capital stock which imposes a limit to the

Figure IX.3

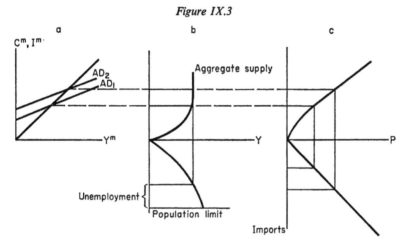

permissible level of output. The capacity level of output is attained long before the labour force is fully utilized. Under these conditions an increase in aggregate monetary demand would merely be inflationary and will exacerbate balance of payments difficulties. This situation is summarized in the composite diagram of Figure IX.3. Part (a) depicts a conventional Keynesian increase in aggregate monetary expenditures. In Part (b) the monetary level of national income is translated into real terms by the aggregate supply function whilst the lower portion of the figure shows the output–employment relationship and the extent of unemployment. Finally, Part (c) of the figure gives the relationship between aggregate monetary demand and the price level (drawn for any given capacity real income) and postulates an assumed relationship between the price level and imports (2).

It is Part (b) of the figure which sums up the case against the use of

---

(2) I.e. that the cross-elasticity between imports and domestic goods is positive.

Keynesian policies in the less advanced economies. Here the inelastic portion of the aggregate supply curve is attained long before the full employment level of the labour force is reached. In contrast, in the advanced industrial economy, the causal relationship is usually reversed. It is the attainment of full employment of the labour force which imposes a limit to the sustainable output level and may lead to balance of payments problems.

Whether the less advanced economies face such supply limitations must remain an empirical issue which cannot be determined *a priori*. Even if supply conditions are more elastic than has usually been supposed, the application of standard Keynesian remedies may not necessarily be appropriate or capable of being carried out. For example, it is sometimes argued that there is frequently excess capacity in manufacturing industry in developing countries and that in consequence both output and employment could be increased, i.e. there is no trade-off problem between output and employment, if demand were increased for manufacturing products by some form of fiscal action. It turns out that this is quite a complex analytical and policy problem. In this context, it will be sufficient to illustrate the complexities by showing how much information would need to be in the hands of the fiscal authorities, if suitable action is contemplated.

Consider the case in which the fiscal measure used to increase output is a straight output subsidy, and the supply curves of the relevant industries subsidized are completely elastic over the relevant range. In addition there is another set of 'industries', e.g. agriculture and services, whose supply curves are completely inelastic (a strong assumption of course) in the short run. The models developed in Chapter IV may be recalled at this juncture, for these give some indications of the direction of the changes which would result from fiscal action and the 'side effects' which would follow:

1. The 'first round effect' of a subsidy would appear to be an increase in output and demand for labour, but the *extent* of the increase will depend on the price elasticity of demand for manufacturing goods. Even if the effect is positive, an increase in the demand for labour does not necessarily lead to an increase in the demand for numbers employed. The assumption that all labour is homogeneous is implicit in the suggestion that demand for labour

means increase in numbers employed, whereas the actual situation in developing countries may be nearer one in which there are shortages of skilled labour for manufacturing. Therefore, even if the first round effect means that demand for labour increases, much more needs to be known about the nature of the labour input required, as well as labour hiring policies generally, before any conclusion could be drawn.

2. The 'second round effects' can be dichotomized into the various injections and leakages which are illustrated in the models in Chapter IV. The rise in total output will cause a corresponding rise in *incomes* with consequential positive multiplier effects which feed back through consumption expenditure to increase demand for both agricultural and manufacturing products. The fiscal authorities clearly have to know what the income elasticities of demand are for the various sectors, both in order to know whether the changes are having the desired effects and, incidentally, in order to be able to calculate the required amount of subsidy. If we adopt the assumption used in Chapter IV of equi-proportional consumption in the two sectors, then all demand curves will move to the right. In the case of manufacturing, by assumption, output and demand for labour input will further increase. In the case of the other sectors, again by assumption, the effect will be a rise in prices, i.e. the domestic 'terms of trade' will move in favour of these sectors.

3. There are similar effects, which would have to be calculated in the case of the changes in demand produced through the inter-industry system. One effect of interdependency in the economy is that agricultural inputs for industry will rise in price, so that the output-promoting effects of the subsidy to manufacturing will be offset by the rise in variable costs. Another is that leakages would 'soften' the domestic impact of the subsidy change, assuming that the tax system is flexible enough to 'pick up' revenue as domestic output expands, e.g. through corporation taxes and income tax collected at source, and also assuming that imports are allowed to expand. Again, measurement would require a calculation of the income elasticity of both taxes and demand for imports.

4. There would be further effects which are not discernible in the input–output system. These would increase: (i) the effects of the change in relative prices of manufactured and other goods and

services on demand and on the general price level; (ii) the effects on the economy of the alternative methods of financing the subsidy which are open to the government.

Now let us review the use of fiscal policy to create employment in the circumstances just described, bearing in mind the kind of policy context we have in mind. *Firstly*, it is not certain *a priori* that employment in terms of labour units would increase, so that much more would need to be known about the nature of the industrial conditions obtaining in any particular developing country before one could be sure that fiscal instruments would achieve the desired aim. *Secondly*, there is quite a long list of assumptions to be formulated and tested in order to analyse both the direction and magnitude of change. An input–output table for the economy is essential, but we may recall from Chapter IV that the use of such a table is limited by the assumption of proportionality in the inter-industry system, an assumption which it is not possible to make when the very nature of the situation we are interested in requires differing elasticities of supply. *Thirdly*, even if the full effects on employment and the side effects can be calculated, the degree of 'fine tuning' in the fiscal system necessary to produce the desired result while minimizing the side effects is almost certainly not possible in many developing countries.

If it is conceded that supply conditions are inelastic so that policies to promote employment are not accompanied by any notable increase in physical output, then we are at once faced with a cruel dilemma. For attempts at employment creation will normally entail less efficient modes of production than would otherwise obtain; this is particularly true of the public sector. If the public sector is deliberately made more labour-intensive in order to raise employment levels it is reasonable to conclude that the per-unit cost of output will thereby be raised. As long as the government sector faces a budget constraint, the implication must be that employment creation policies will be accompanied by a decrease in total output. Indeed, this conclusion is implicit in the attempt to depart from the factor-mix combination determined by profit-maximizing motives in the private sector. It follows that, the more that resources are transferred from the private to the public sector, the greater will be the level of employment but the lower will be total output; per capita income must fall. We have a clear example of trade-off which we summarize in Figure IX.4.

In Figure IX.4, the line NN' represents the total population which may seek employment either in the public or the private sector. National income is maximized when all employed resources are solely allocated in the private sector but extensive unemployment results indicated by *b*. Unemployment is minimized by a policy of transferring all employable resources to the public sector, $b > a$, but this also implies the minimal income level. The nature of the trade-off is simply the extent to which national income must be given up in order to obtain an increment to the total numbers employed.

Figure IX.4

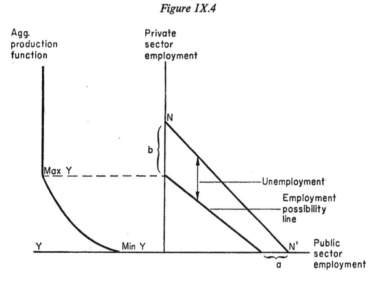

However, the question of trade-off is more complex than this. The cost of employment creation will in all probability involve a decrease in the rate of growth. This follows from a number of considerations. First, the decline in the level of per capita income will normally reduce the pace of capital formation. This will be reinforced if labour-intensive methods of production increase the percentage of resources flowing to labour and away from the owners of capital and if saving propensities differ between the respective income classes

(3). Secondly, quite apart from any adverse impacts upon capital formation, the adoption of more labour-intensive methods may slow the pace of technological change since the latter is generally associated with an increase in the amount of capital per capita.

Other considerations could be allowed to enter the analysis. For example, we might wish to consider the impact of employment creation upon the balance of payments, the rate of population growth and so forth. For present purposes, however, it is sufficient to deal with our joint trade-off—the short-term decline in per capita income upon the one hand and the fall in the long-term growth rate upon the other. In doing so we are taking an important step towards an understanding of the decision-making process where both policy objectives and conflicts are numerous. Our previous examples dealt with two conflicting policy objectives implying only one trade-off. By dealing with the case of a multiple trade-off we are able theoretically to generalize the analysis to the real-world situation where society's welfare function encompasses any number of interreacting policy goals and conflicts. Whilst the mathematical analysis is more complex no new principles are required.

We may illustrate the nature of our dual dilemma by reference to the three-dimensional diagram of Figure IX.5. The left-hand section of the figure portrays the trade-off between increased employment and income per capita, whilst the right-hand segment depicts a similar situation between increased employment and economic growth. The solid thus described shows all possible combinations of higher employment, per capita income and long-term economic growth. We may imagine a series of community indifference curves emanating from the origin and progressively slicing the solid until a tangency solution between the community indifference curve and the conical surface is attained. Any further indifference curve is theoretically unattainable. The tangency solution maximizes the welfare of society. We may carry the analysis a stage further, however, by postulating a minimum level of income per capita which is politically

---

(3) Although consideration of the Cobb–Douglas production function would suggest that greater labour intensity would not change the respective income shares of labour and capital. This, however, is to assume all adjustments are frictionless and to ignore any short-term deviations from the long-term ultimate solution.

acceptable, and likewise by assuming a minimal growth rate which is deemed feasible in the light of all other conditions. The two are, of course, interrelated in that a rate of growth of income in excess of population expansion automatically leads to a raising of income per capita and vice versa.

Figure IX.5

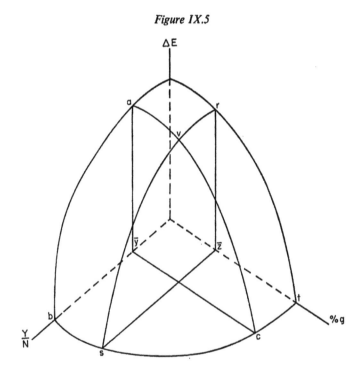

Let us assume that the minimal level of income per capita is given by $\bar{y}$, and the lowest acceptable rate of growth by $\bar{z}$. Lower values of y and z are inadmissible when considering the social welfare function. Alternatively, we may say that minimal values are imposed upon the constraints which then delimit the feasible range of policy action.

The effect of imposing the minimal income level $\bar{y}$ reduces the permissible surface of the solid to the area *abc*. Likewise the impact of adopting a minimal growth rate $\bar{z}$ implies that only the surface *rst* is available to policy action. The combined constraint thus reduces the scope of permissible policy action to the area *vsc*.

More formally, our objective function is represented by
[$u = u(N, y, z)$, where u is again the ordinal utility index and is maximized subject to the dual constraint

$$y \geqslant \bar{y}, z \geqslant \bar{z}.$$

Having indicated the nature of the problem what is the scope for fiscal policy? As we have already shown, once the decision has been taken to render the public sector more labour-intensive, enlarging the size of the public sector *vis-à-vis* the private sector will raise the aggregate numbers employed. Thus even though an increase in aggregate monetary demand by itself has no effect on the numbers employed it is still permissible to assume that a balanced budget fiscal change has positive employment generating impacts. Thus

$$dN = \frac{\partial N}{\partial G} dG + \frac{\partial N}{\partial T} dT > 0$$

where T is the tax yield and G the volume of government expenditures. Secondly, the fiscal system may be utilized to change the existing pattern of comparative factor prices in favour of labour-intensive methods, and discriminate against capital-absorbing techniques within the private sector. Taxes may be imposed upon capital equipment and selective employment taxes adapted to subsidize the employment of labour. Such measures may be supplemented by wage, import and price controls designed to favour activities which are naturally more labour-intensive. Thus even though Keynesian measures may be inappropriate it is still the case that the employment level will respond to fiscal incentives.

Likewise, fiscal policy may be used to mitigate the force of the constraints by increasing incentives to save, by stimulating techno-logical advance and perhaps also by social policies which render lower per-capita income levels more acceptable to society as a whole. Diagrammatically, such influences would serve to change the curvature of the trade-off slopes and enlarge the permissible area of policy action. Alternatively fiscal variables enter into the objective function and are part of the means by which the utility index is maximized. We do not need to pursue the now familiar technique of the Lagrange multiplier to determine the outcome; without specifying the functional relationships more precisely we are not able to advance the analysis beyond our diagrammatic framework.

We do not mean to simplify the tremendous problems facing the emergent nations by suggesting that fiscal policy may solve all difficulties; all that we have proposed in the present example is that fiscal variables must be given due notice in the maximization procedure. Our purpose in the present illustration has been to show that the question of decision-making need not be confined to a Keynesian framework nor is it confined to a dual objective policy problem. Goals, conflicts, and instruments are manifold. The purpose of the present volume has been merely to indicate the place and importance of the fiscal variable in the complex schema of economic decision-making.

V. INTER-TEMPORAL UTILITY MAXIMIZATION AND FISCAL POLICY

Thus far our analysis of the use of fiscal policy in maximizing a social-welfare function has assumed that we are interested in some terminal position which, given the shape of the utility function, the boundary conditions and technical constraints, is the best conceivable. Time does not enter into the utility function or into the examination of the process of adjustment of the fiscal system to reach the 'bliss' point. We have shown in Chapter VI that the introduction of time and the introduction of lagged responses in the system modifies policy prescriptions. It seems worth investigating how far lagged responses also complicate the whole question of community choices with regard both to objectives and instruments.

Let us use a very simple example. Let us assume that a particular fiscal 'mix' of taxes and expenditures obtains which results in a growth pattern of national output depicted by curve A_1 in Figure IX.6. The substitution of another 'mix' produces an alternative pattern which is represented by curve A_2. Which is the 'best' mix? To answer this question, the economist must ask the policy-maker a series of questions:

(a) What is the nature of the objective function? Is the policy maker solely interested in growth in national output or are other objectives to be considered? Let us assume for the moment that the answer is that the policy-maker is interested solely in growth.

(b) Curve A_1 produces more output in the near future as compared with A_2, but less in the future. How does the policy-maker view output as a function of time? The accepted way of comparing present with future utilities is, of course, to select some discount rate, and it would be reasonable to assume that this rate is positive denoting that the present value of a unit of output in the future is less than the present value of a unit of output now.

(c) What time horizon is relevant? The policy-maker may have no interest in the effects of fiscal policy in the remote future when he may not be in office, or when changes in the shape of the objective function take place. In other words, after some point in time the value of future output is nil, i.e. the rate of discount is infinite, and to compare present with future output, we must assume that the objective or utility function is stable.

Figure IX.6

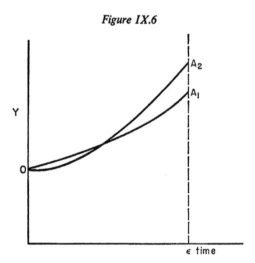

We can now specify the objective function as follows:

$$\pi_0(Y_i) = \sum_{n=1}^{\varepsilon} \frac{\pi_n(Y_i)}{(1+i)^n}$$

where ε is some limit set to the time horizon in 'years', $0 < i < 1$ is a social time preference rate, e.g. 0·05 or 5 per cent.

The policy-maker having specified n, and i, the two alternative fiscal policies can be ranked. However, while the example illustrates some important features of the problem of the choice of fiscal policies in a dynamic setting, it is not on all fours with the previous analysis. We have *ranked* two alternative fiscal policies, but not maximized the function. Once we begin to think of maximizing the present value of future output, it is clear that the objective function is far out of line with a policy-making situation, for it is inconceivable that in any community one would maximize output regardless of other objectives. At the very least, one would want to introduce as Section III above indicates, a consumption constraint, for the policy-maker must consider the social implications of a fiscal policy which would be required to transfer a large proportion of total resources to capital formation at the expense of current consumption per head.

The example chosen is merely illustrative. In actual planning models which fix the pattern of thinking about policy problems, particularly in developing countries, an attempt is made to grapple with the problems of the real world by devising much more complicated objective functions, and using multi-sector growth models of a high degree of sophistication, all within a dynamic framework. The reader must take it on trust that even an exercise in comparative statics involving only two time periods, a simple two-sector growth model and two 'arguments' (i.e. the 'O.K.' terminology for the elements in the objective function) requires the use of mathematical techniques which are beyond the scope of this work, and also lead us into untrodden ways so far as the fiscal economists are concerned. Until public finance has come more to terms with these new developments, we can avoid troubling the reader with a further input of economic theory with a (fairly) clear conscience (4)!

---

(4) The interested (and mathematically versatile) reader may obtain a taste of these complications by consulting Louis Lefeber, 'Planning in a Surplus Labour Economy', *American Economic Review*, Vol. LVIII, June 1968. This article makes specific reference to the use of tax/subsidy policy for increasing employment in developing countries.

Chapter X

FROM THEORY TO PRACTICE

I. INTRODUCTION

The analysis we have developed in the previous chapters is or should be part of the technical equipment of economists who are employed by those governments who feel a commitment to fulfil the objectives which have been specified at various points in the argument. The reader should be aware, if he is not so already, that the practical application of the analysis calls upon a range of further expertise beyond that of logical statements expressed in mathematical form. It may be argued that, at this juncture, the fiscal theorist should now bow his way off the stage and at most wave his hand by way of introduction towards those ready to perform the next act in the drama of marrying theory to policy. However, as the seeds of the future development of any drama lie in its beginnings, so is it possible, and perhaps useful, to show the reader how the tasks of the statistician, econometrist and budget planner can be related to the model-building process.

Let us consider a very simple example which defines these additional tasks for policy application. Assume, and we have already explained that this is a very simple assumption, that what the government is interested in is the stabilization of the level of money national income at some specified level. To know what level it is desired to reach, it is important to know the existing level over, say, the past seven years, in order to define both its magnitude and trend. Furthermore, as the value of national income is influenced by the decisions of households, firms and government, we must have full knowledge of their transactions with one another. In short, a full range of social accounting information must be at the disposal of policy-makers. We discuss the social accounting requirements of fiscal policy in Section II of this chapter.

As frequently emphasized in this work (particularly in Chapter VII), the problem of stabilizing the level of national income is one of choosing the 'right' values of the fiscal parameters to influence the decisions of the private sector. An economic forecast must be made which specifies how national income will be developed on the assumption of *no change* in the fiscal parameters and then, on the basis of the forecast, to decide on the correct adjustment to be made to them. A glance at, say, equation VII.1 indicates that such a forecast must be based on the calculation of the values of the parameters. This is the task of the econometrist, and Section III describes the procedure adopted in measuring fiscal performance with the use of quantitative techniques.

Assuming that it is known what values the fiscal parameters should take in order to achieve the single chosen objective, then suitable forms of fiscal control must be found. It is worth reminding ourselves that the model deployed in Chapter II shows the importance of integrating monetary and fiscal policy, so that it will be relevant also to consider the nature of the controls over the monetary system in the same context. The development of new institutional devices which further the aims of fiscal policy is one of the most important tasks of the fiscal or budget planner, and one which deserves more credit than it often gets in academic economic circles. We have therefore devoted a little space to a description of some of these devices, and the problems which beset policy co-ordination. This is the subject of the penultimate Section IV of this chapter.

II. A BRIEF REVIEW OF THE SOCIAL ACCOUNTING REQUIRE-MENTS OF FISCAL POLICY

It is beyond the scope of this work to describe the problems encountered in collecting and collating statistics of national income and its components and the relevant financial statistics for the study of trends in monetary variables (1). The point to be made at this stage is to offer the warning that even governments completely committed to quantitative analysis of the economy and willing to invest consider-

---

(1) The interested reader is referred to *National Accounts Statistics: Sources and Methods*, ed. Rita Maurice, CSO Studies in Official Statistics, No. 13, 1968.

M

able resources in statistical work are still in the position where they
only have a very approximate idea of the value of the main aggregates
in the year preceding the chosen planning period. This is because of
the immense difficulties of obtaining accurate data quickly.

This section of the work is more concerned with the *classification*
(2) of the social accounts for purposes of economic analysis designed
to further the aims of short and long-run stabilization.

So far as economic stability is concerned, the emphasis is on the
classification of transactions of the government with a view to
determining their direct or indirect effect on aggregate income and

Table X.1. Identity Matrix of Income Transactions

Payments ↓ → Receipts	Firms	House-holds	Govern-ment	Capital A/C	Total
Firms	—	C_h	G_c+I_g / G_w	I_p	y^m
Households	y^f	—	R	—	y^h
Government	T_t-G_s / $T_{y(f)}$	$T_{y(h)}$	—	—	G_r
Capital A/C	S_f	S_h	S_g	—	S_r
Total	y^m	y^h	G_p	I	—

other target variables and this requires us not only to classify
government transactions in a form which identifies them as part of
national income and expenditure, but also to display their influence
on those components of national income and expenditure which
reflect the decisions of the private sector. We can derive such a
classification from a simple identity matrix (see Table X.1). For the
sake of simplicity, we assume a closed economy.

(2) Cf. also the system of regional accounts classification in Chapter IV.

The identity matrix in this simple form produces three sector accounts, and an (implicit) capital account:

I. FIRMS' ACCOUNT

+	−
1. Sales of goods and services to households (C_h)	5. Payments of factor incomes (Y^f)
2. Sales of current goods and services to government (G_c)	6. Payments of taxes on expenditure *less* government subsidies $(T_t - G_s)$
3. Sales of new capital goods to government (I_p)	7. Payment of direct taxes on firms $(T_{y(f)})$
4. Wages and salaries of public administration (G_w)	8. Firms' saving, including depreciation (S_f)

Firms' receipts ≡ National expenditure at market prices (Y^m)	Firms' payments ≡ National income at market prices (Y^m)

II. HOUSEHOLDS' ACCOUNT

+	−
9. (= 5). Receipts of factor incomes (Y^f)	11. (= 1). Purchases of Goods and services (C_h)
10. Transfers from government (R) (i) Social security payments (ii) Debt interest	12. Taxes on income $(T_{y(h)})$ 13. Households' saving, including depreciation (S_h)

Households' receipts (Y^h) ≡ Personal income before tax	Households' payments (Y^h)

III. GOVERNMENT ACCOUNT

+	−
14. (= 7+12). Taxes on income	16. (= 2+3+4). Government expenditure on goods and services
(a) Taxes on personal income $(T_{y(h)})$	(a) Expenditure on current goods and services (G_c)
(b) Taxes on corporate income $(T_{y(f)})$	(b) Expenditure on wages and salaries of public administration (G_w)

	(c) Expenditure on capital goods (I_g)
15. (= 6). Taxes on expenditure (T_i) – subsidies (G_r)	17. (= 10). Transfers (R)
	18. Government saving (including depreciation) (S_g)

Government receipts (G_r)	Government payments (G_p)

Before examining the implications of the identity matrix for budgetary rules and classification, a little more needs to be said about a few problems obscured by the simplicity of the presentation.

1. In order to fit our accounts to the requirements of the identity matrix, we have to ignore quite deliberately that, in practice, *all* the main decision-makers may pursue *all* the main activities of production, consumption and adding to wealth, instead of ascribing, for example, production solely to firms, and consumption to households and government. However, this complication does not affect the principles governing the division of the budget nor budgetary rules.

2. Certain accounting problems are ignored. For example, if the interest in the accounts centres in the correct total of GNP, then government expenditure should include not only purchases of goods and services, but also an imputed amount for the rent of government-owned buildings. However, so far as stabilization policy is concerned, such an item has no significance at all. In practice, this item in any case is balanced by a receipt on income account so that the total government surplus is not affected by this accounting device. Another example relates to the problem of drawing up accounts on an accrual as distinct from a cash basis.

3. All intra-sector transactions have been ignored. Two observations may be made about this omission. The first is that the 'government' we are interested in, broadly defined, is the central government. It follows that any presentation of the budget accounts suitable for stabilization policy would have to show the grants and other payments made to other layers of government which, broadly speaking, cannot pursue anti-cyclical policy, but which, nevertheless, may have their activities influenced by the central government in a way which will promote stabilization (cf. Chapter IV, above).

Thus some modification is needed to allow for this, even in a set of 'model' accounts. The second observation relates to the type of forecasting model used into which government transactions are fitted. The more the model is disaggregated, the more it is necessary to show more detail in the government budget accounts. For example, if a disaggregated model takes account of inter-industry transactions, it follows that government expenditure on goods and services must be disaggregated to show their industrial origin. In the example given above, we have only two sectors shown: the 'public administration sector' and the 'rest of industry'. Similarly, the taxes on final output, e.g. sales taxes, might be divided according to the tax payments by different industrial sectors. Neither of these observations, however, affect the budget division or the 'rules' governing the accrual of surpluses or deficits.

4. If we wish to extend the analysis of the influence of government transactions to cover the effects of government surpluses or deficits on the structure of financial transactions, we should extend it to include a 'flow-of-funds' system. For example, if the money supply were affected by such transaction, then any stabilization policy would have to allow for this. In principle, what is required is a classification of financial transactions which is relevant for stabilization policy, for example, according to the time structure of loans made to and by the government. In addition, the links would have to be forged between the government and the other sectors. Flow-of-funds analysis of the standard kind would require a somewhat different classification of sectors which would specifically identify the commercial and central banking systems.

5. Having agreed to confine the accounts to those of the central government, there is still the problem encountered in defining the government. While the traditional emphasis on control of expenditure would not necessarily require that all funds administered by the government need be shown in the budget, the pursuit of economic stability demands the appraisal of the importance of extra-budgetary receipts and payments as an element in income determination. Indeed, with the development of comprehensive social security schemes in several European countries, particular attention has been paid not only to the effects of such schemes on the distribution of income but also on its creation.

The existence of such extra-budgetary funds at least demands the identification of the relevant income and financial flows, but whether these funds themselves should be consolidated with the main budget accounts very much depends upon the extent to which they can be made the effective instruments of stabilization policy when they may be designed mainly for other purposes, e.g. income support by social security funds. If extra-budgetary funds are included, they will naturally affect the size and composition of the budget and also the size of the deficit or surplus. Moreover, to the extent that they are designed to meet other objectives of policy, they may follow different budgetary rules. For example, if a social security scheme is supposed to embody actuarial principles or is self-balancing, this may place a limitation on the use of 'formula flexibility' (to use the Musgravian term) which would only be operative if changes in contributions and benefits (and therefore discretionary changes in the annual surplus and deficit) were permissible.

We are now in a position to present the kind of budget accounts which would fit the requirements of a policy of economic stabilization *as derived from a macroeconomic theory of income determination.* We underline the latter half of the last sentence in order to emphasize that as theories are extended, modified or even discarded, so also must the classification and form of budget accounts be changed. Table X.2 must also be regarded as a minimum requirement which ignores some important complications of the real world, notably the exclusion of foreign transactions, but it can be assumed that these complications do not alter the argument in any essential way.

The contrast of the stabilization budget accounts with the 'traditional' ones may now be drawn. Apart from obvious differences in the classification of individual items, the division of the budget is drawn with expenditure on newly created capital goods firmly placed 'above the line', because, whatever their effect on the net worth position of the government, they are an important element in aggregate demand influenced by government fiscal action. Indeed, the net worth position is irrelevant, and so are the traditional budgetary rules about current balance, if the main object of budgetary action is to achieve stability. The magnitude of government budget surpluses and deficits is the outcome of the national budget which will determine the role of the government budget in making the

Table X.2. Classification of Budget Accounts for Economic Stability

---

INCOME ACCOUNT

+	−
1. Taxes on income	4. Government expenditure on goods and services
(a) Taxes on personal income	(a) Purchases from industrial sector, x_1
(b) Taxes on corporate income	Purchases from industrial sector, x_2
(c) Other taxes on income	. . . .
	Purchases from industrial sector, x_n
2. Taxes on expenditure	(b) Capital formation
Taxes paid by industrial sector, x_1	
Taxes paid by industrial sector, x_2	5. Transfers to households
. . . .	6. Subsidies to firms to industrial sector, x_1
Taxes paid by industrial sector, x_n	Subsidies to firms to industrial sector, x_2
3. Interest and other income	. . . .
(a) From households	Subsidies to firms to industrial sector, x_n
(b) From firms	7. Government saving (including depreciation)

FINANCIAL ACCOUNT

8. (= 7). Government saving (including depreciation)	11. Lending (*less* repayments by government)
9. Borrowing (*less* repayments to government)	(a) Short term
(a) Short term	(b) Long term
(b) Long term	12. Net increase in cash holdings
10. Liquidation of assets (*less* purchase of existing assets)	

---

projected movements in the economy consistent with the stability objective. Moreover, it follows that the relevant surplus or deficit is not the traditional current surplus or deficit but the 'overall' surplus or deficit, or what is sometimes called the cash surplus or deficit.

It is sometimes maintained that the stability 'rule' requires the accumulation of overall surpluses in periods of incipient inflation and deficits in periods of incipient depression, with a rough balance over the cycle. The implication of this position is that the balanced budget, as classified above, is in some sense 'neutral' with respect to changes in overall demand. There are two reasons why this may not be the case. Differing *compositions* of income receipts and payments with a balanced budget in all cases would not have the same multiplier effects, and a multiplier of zero would only be one of a large number of possible cases. Secondly, no allowance is being made for the structure of financial flows which even if they are the same amount in aggregate on both sides of the account, may have very different effects on aggregate demand either directly or indirectly through changes in interest rates, depending on their magnitude. Thus the sale of assets which is balanced by an increase in cash holdings will have a very different effect from one which is balanced by increased lending to the private sector.

Considering growth policy, the general criterion of classification of the budget accounts is to distinguish between those transactions which promote and those which inhibit growth. As the forces which determine growth are unlikely to operate without considerable lags, and as growth is rarely spectacular over the very short period, it also follows that the analysis of budget accounts with a view to determining their influence on growth requires consideration of a time period of longer than one year. Hence the popularity of linking budget projections with economic plans for five or even ten years.

Generally speaking, the promotion of growth, as our models in Chapter VI affirm, is associated with changes in the amount and composition of capital investment, both public and private, defining capital in a very broad way in order to include human capital formation. It is clear that this preoccupation with capital formation, even in the broad sense, may be questionable. Changes in labour supply and effort and in technology, as is clear from recent econometric studies, are not negligible forces in determining the pace and pattern of growth and may be influenced appreciably by government tax and expenditure patterns. While this may be so, it is difficult to ascertain the influence of such forces on budgetary classification and rules, while it is somewhat easier to suggest changes in budget accounts which follow from the preoccupation with investment policy. It may be useful to offer a digression on the distinction between the proposed classification in Table X.3 below and 'traditional' ideas of a capital budget which have had a new lease of life in recent budgetary discussion (3):

1. The ultimate object of policy is the promotion and growth of the economy and not the 'soundness' of the net-worth position of the government. This means that it is just as important to identify those activities of the government which alter the amount and composition of investment in the *private* sector as in the public sector.

2. It follows that a general distinction between current and capital expenditure is too crude for our purpose. Clearly, investment in human capital and in social overhead capital must be included and, further, a clear distinction must be made between new capital formation directly made by the government and induced by the government and the mere transfer of assets from the public to the private sector and vice versa. Going a stage further, the *method* of including new capital formation or transfer, e.g. loans, grants, state shareholding, etc., needs to be clearly shown.

3. Even if the policy of growth promotion embodies sophisticated criteria in order to determine whether or not a particular project should be undertaken or financed by the government, such as those associated with cost–benefit analysis, this is not to say that projects, in any narrow financial sense at least, must be self-liquidating or must be financed by particular kinds of receipts. On the other hand, this is not to argue that a consistent growth programme might not contain any recoverable elements in capital expenditure or would not demand, for instance, some form of provisions for the depreciation of government assets. Thus while the 'rules' governing the finance of capital formation might be different, allowance must be made in the classification of budget data for these items.

4. The preoccupation with the general influence of the budget on growth suggests once again that the links forged by government transactions with other sectors must be clearly shown. At a minimum, therefore, government transactions must be subdivided by the

(3) Cf., for example, the symposium in the *Review of Economics and Statistics* May, 1963.

Table X.3. Classification of Budget Accounts for Economic Growth

INCOME ACCOUNT

+ | −

1. Taxes on income

2. Taxes on expenditure

3. Interest and other income

4. Government expenditure on current goods and services
5. Transfers
6. Subsidies
7. Government saving (including depreciation)

CAPITAL ACCOUNT

8. (= 7). Government saving (including depreciation)

9. Borrowing (*less* repayments to government)

10. Liquidation of assets

11. Other capital receipts

12. Expenditure on physical capital formation
    (a) Direct expenditure
    (b) Indirect expenditure
        (i) loans
            —to other government layers
        (ii) capital grants
            —to other government layers
            —to private sector
        (iii) other indirect, e.g. financial investment
13. Expenditure on non-physical capital formation
    (a) Direct expenditure
    (b) Indirect expenditure
        (i) loans
            —to other government layers
            —to private sector
        (ii) grants
            —to other government layers
            —to private sector
        (iii) other indirect
14. Purchase of existing assets
    (a) Direct
    (b) Indirect
        (i) loans
        (ii) grants
15. Repayments of loans by government
16. Net increase in cash holdings

relevant sectors, both private and other public (such as states within a federation or local government units within a unitary state). In a really elaborate system, a complete disaggregation of the combined capital account (see Table X.1) is called for. This is a tall order if one is concerned with budget projections, and in any case, even if only nominal figures can be inserted in the projections, governments might be unwise to publish them because of their possible effect on the capital and foreign exchange markets. This would be a classic case of a projection resulting in the alteration of the data on which the projections are based.

Table X.3 is illustrative rather than exhaustive, and is designed only to highlight differences from previous classifications and divisions in the budget accounts. An important example of amplification of Table X.3 might be the combination of an object and perhaps a functional classification with an economic classification so that the benefits and costs of particular investment programmes might be more clearly discerned.

Manifestly, the classifications and divisions of the budget which seem to fit best with 'newer' policies pursued by fiscal means are different from those suggested by 'traditional' policies. Also the main budget rule is *consistency* with the projections in which the objectives of policy are clearly stated in quantifiable form (so far as this is possible), the equations of the relevant model satisfactorily solved, and their parameters correctly estimated. No simple rule of budgetary balance can be derived from this procedure.

This conclusion is hardly surprising to a generation of specialists who have studied the theory of fiscal policy as an integral part of the study of public finance. What may be lost sight of in the enthusiasm for sophisticated social accounting is the essential difference, relatively small maybe as compared with the difference between 'new' and 'old' budgeting, between classification and division of the budget for stability on the one hand and growth on the other. Furthermore, as theories of stability and growth become further refined and their applications become more extensive, so too will accounting changes be necessary.

The only sensible conclusion would appear to be that, after allowing for the opportunity cost of specialized statistical services of the

kind required to implement government budgeting (and the opportunity cost can be high in developing countries), there is no reason
why all these classifications should not be made and used and why
any single one should dominate the scene, given the pursuit of the
policies described. We must beware of replacing new orthodoxies for
old and therefore of any social accounting scheme embodying
government transactions which claims to replace all those already in
existence. Perhaps this point is overlooked by some of those anxious
to achieve international acceptance of one and only one system of
budgetary classification and division.

III. MEASURING FISCAL PERFORMANCE

(a) Theory

Having sorted out the identities which form up the income equation
and traced the links between the decision-makers in the economy in a
social-accounting schema, the next problem is to measure the
impact of the system of public finance on the economy. In order to
perform this operation, those appointed to advise the Minister of
Finance or relevant senior politician in charge of economic policy
must commission studies which indicate the *total* impact of the
budget on the relevant target variables, and the effects of a *marginal
change* in one or more of the fiscal parameters. It is necessary to know
the total impact mainly in order to gain perspective in the pursuit of
fiscal policy, although policy situations will normally require only
marginal adjustments.

Again for the sake of simplicity, let us concentrate on fiscal
efforts to control the level of national income. Consider a simple
macrostatic model, very similar to equation III.1, for a single open
economy.

$$Y = C + I + G + (X - M)$$
$$C = bY^d$$

where Y^d = Disposable income.

$$M = jY^d$$
$$Y^d = Y(1 - t_y) + R - \eta$$

where t_y is a proportional income tax rate, R = transfers and n =
taxes invariant with respect to income.

I, G, X, R and n are assumed to be autonomous
$$0<b, j, t_y<1$$
The solving for Y by the usual method, we have:

$$Y = \bar{I}+\bar{G}+\bar{X}+(b-j)(\bar{R}-\bar{\eta})\cdot\frac{1}{1-(b-j)(1-t_y)} \qquad \text{(X.1)}$$

We can distinguish three budgetary effects on the level of national income (Y). The first is the *impact* or *first-round effect*: This is given by the value of government transactions in the multiplicand:

$$\bar{G}+(b-j)\bar{R}-(b-j)\bar{\eta} \qquad . \qquad . \qquad \text{(X.2)}$$

It will be noted that there are three components, government purchases of goods and services, transfers, and taxes, which can be correspondingly identified in the government accounts (see Table X.1). However, in practice, we would identify a greater range of transactions, as Table X.1 already indicates. Put more formally, the first round effect may be written as:

$$J = \sum_{i=1}^{n}(a_iG_i)+\sum_{j=1}^{n}(a_jF_j) \qquad . \qquad . \qquad \text{(X.3)}$$

where G_i is the ith government expenditure and F_j is the jth method of finance. The as are weights which indicate the first round impact of the individual terms. Putting equation X.2 in terms of equation X.3, the appropriate weight for G is clearly 1, and for $\bar{R}$ and $\bar{n}$, less than 1 as $0<b, j<1$. Thus assuming $b = \cdot9$ and $j = \cdot15$, the $a_R = \cdot75$.

The second is the *total* effect of the budget. This is obtained by multiplying the impact effect by the *multiplier*, which, in our example, is given by

$$k = 1\Big/1-(b-j)(1-t_y)$$

The total effect is measured by the expression $J.k$, assuming $t_y = \cdot10$, then $k = 3\cdot1$ (approx.).

The third case (4) is the effect of *discretionary* changes or *marginal*

---

(4) One might identify as a fourth case 'built-in flexibility'. It is certainly true that a good deal of attention has been paid to the measurement of the built-in flexibility of fiscal systems. However, in this context we are more interested in economic measurement which acts as an aid to 'positive' fiscal action involving changes in fiscal parameters. Some institutional aspects of the need to improve automatic stabilizers are dealt with later. See Section IV of this Chapter.

changes. These occur, as already explained, when one or more of the
fiscal parameters are altered to offset 'undesirable' expected changes
in the other parameters in the system. Chapters II and III already
explain how we express discretionary changes in marginal form.
Hence:

$$\frac{\partial Y}{\partial G} = k, \frac{\partial Y}{\partial R} = (b-j) \cdot k, \frac{\partial Y}{\partial \eta} = -(b-j) \cdot k,$$

$$\frac{\partial Y}{\partial t_y} = -(b-j) \cdot k^{-2}$$

where, as before, the multiplier, $k = \dfrac{1}{1-(b-j)(1-t_y)}$

(b) Findings

The most comprehensive recent study of the measurement of the
stabilization performance of the budget is that of Bent Hansen
(assisted by Wayne W. Snyder) (5) which was prepared for OECD.
Only some of the general features of this study can be pointed out in
this review. Using a more comprehensive model than that employed
in the previous section—including, for example, indirect taxes—the
authors calculated the *average* values for the relevant coefficients used
in the multiplier analysis, and then calculated the total, discretionary
and automatic effects of the budget on the *volume* of GNP for 7
OECD developed countries.

These measurements were then used to ask a number of questions,
the most important of which concerned the influence of the budget on
trend increase in GNP. Taking for each country the actual annual
rate of increase of GNP over the decade 1955–65, a hypothetical
annual rate of increase of GNP was devised, simply by subtracting
the estimated effects of the budget for each individual year from the
actual rate of increase. Regression analysis was used in order to

---

(5) See their *Fiscal Policy in Seven Countries, 1955–65*, OECD, Paris, March
1969, especially Chapters 1 and 2. For similar studies see, for example,
Richard A. and Peggy B. Musgrave, 'Fiscal Policy', *Britain's Economic
Prospects*, The Brookings Institution, Washington, 1968, and Elliott Morss
and Alan Peacock, 'Measuring the Economic Impact of the Budget in
Developing Countries', *Quantitative Analysis in Public Finance* (edited by
Alan T. Peacock assisted by Dieter Biehl), New York, 1969.

compute the hypothetical and actual trend, and the difference is given as the statistical expression of the 'pure cycle' (6), i.e. actual GNP growth *minus* total or discretionary effects of the budget. In order to estimate the stabilizing effects of the budget, a coefficient of short-term stabilization was devised in order to express the deviations of the actual and hypothetical rates from the trend rate (average GNP growth rate). If stabilization were perfect, then the actual rate

Figure X.1

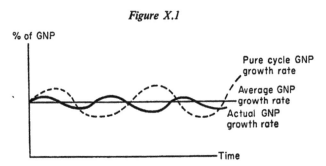

of GNP increase would lie on the trend line, and the value of the coefficient, expressed in percentage terms, would be 100. The smaller the percentage, the less the stabilizing effect, but so long as the percentage is positive, the actual rate of increase would be on balance 'nearer' the trend line than the hypothetical 'pure cycle' rate of increase. If the coefficient has negative values, the actual rate of GNP increase would be on balance 'further away' from the trend line than the 'pure cycle' rate of increase. Figure X.1 illustrates in extreme form the case of positive but not perfect stabilization.

The results of Hansen and his henchmen are interesting, and one example of them is given in Table X.4. The striking conclusion which emerges is that the country most committed to stabilization policy, the United Kingdom, is unique in having a budget which over a decade de-stabilized the economy, considering both total and discretionary changes (7)!

---

(6) The authors realize that other policy measures, fiscal and non-fiscal, could influence the value of the 'pure cycle' rate of increase, but these are neglected. We return to this point later.

(7) For a full discussion of the findings and explanation which is confirmed by Musgrave and Musgrave, op. cit., see Hansen, op. cit., Chapter 8, 'United Kingdom'.

The short explanation of this result is called for, and we can use it as an opportunity to underscore some of the new analytical points in this volume. First of all, one possible reason for the de-stabilizing nature of the budget lies in the problems encountered in conducting fiscal policy in a dynamic setting (cf. Chapter VII) where planners must not only anticipate future changes in aggregate demand but also allow for lagged effects. It seems to be generally believed that the multiplier effects of budgets work themselves out relatively quickly,

Table X.4. Stabilization of GNP Growth Around Trend: Dampening Effect of Central Government (Including Public Enterprise Investment Transactions) (%)

Country	Period	Total effects	Discretionary measures
Belgium	1955–65	21	5
France	1958–65	13	−35
Germany	1958–65	26	14
Italy	1956–65	15	−17
United Kingdom	1955–65	−13	−10
United States	1955–65	49	17

Source: Bent Hansen, op. cit., Table 2.6, p. 69.
Notes: (1) The German calculations exclude public enterprise investment.
(2) The Italian calculations use non-agricultural GDP at factor cost.

i.e. within the fiscal year, but the evidence is not conclusive (8). It seems fairly certain, however, that the lag in company tax collections in Britain behind actual earning of income had an important de-stabilizing effect. Further, the problem of estimating aggregate demand in the UK is made particularly difficult because of the crucial importance of the balance of payments in income formation, the net value added by exports approaching 20 per cent of the GNP. Chapter III explains how the 'closed economy' model needs to be

(8) For the calculation of lags using simulation analysis, see Gary Fromm and Paul Taubman, *Policy Simulations with an Econometric Model*, Chapters 2 and 3, 1968.

modified in order to understand the logic underlying any calculations, and it is not difficult to understand the planner's difficulties in estimating the value of exports which depend upon the tastes and preferences of overseas customers which are difficult to influence by domestic fiscal measures.

A second factor which helps to explain de-stabilization effects exemplified the problem emphasized in Chapters VIII and IX, viz. the difficulty of achieving two or more targets simultaneously by the use of fiscal policy alone. Thus, throughout the period under review, the combination of a strong political commitment to full employment coupled with heavy defence and welfare commitments placed a major constraint on the use of discretionary budgetary measures. This brings us to the third factor. To the extent that discretionary measures were employed, considerable use was made of indirect taxes, the rates of which could be changed in recent years without the need for legislative action. What might have been gained by the lack of political obstacles to speedy change was lost in the side effects of indirect taxes. In Chapter V, we placed particular emphasis on the fact that in considering the effects of indirect taxes on aggregate demand, one has to consider not only the impact effects working through the changes in real incomes but the induced effects which work through price changes and which may affect aggregate demand through the wage–price sprial.

The Hansen study offers interesting empirical backing to another observation made at a much earlier stage in our analysis in Chapter II. It would enormously simplify budgetary planning if change in aggregate demand produced by the budget could be measured by the size of the overall budget surplus or deficit. Great store has been set, for example, by IMF pundits on the measurement of the budget surplus or deficit for this reason (9). The study shows quite conclusively that the predictions based on 'budget balance' would be quite different. Although we have ourselves emphasized that fiscal effects on aggregate demand depend on what assumptions are made about monetary policy and therefore on the monetary effects of

---

(9) See the now famous article by J. J. Polak, 'Monetary Analysis of Income Formation and Payments Problems', *Staff Papers*, International Monetary Fund, Vol. VI, 1957.

N

budgetary changes, we are bound to agree with the authors that a large question mark hovers over the use of the simplified method of measurement (10).

(c) Problems of statistical estimation

A brief word needs to be said about the problems of statistical estimation. The results so far reported assume, of course, that the problems of estimating the coefficients in the model have been solved. The standard practice adopted in estimation is to use simple regression analysis. For example, an average value for the consumption coefficient (cf. (b) in equation X.1 above) is obtained by finding the linear regression line relating consumption to disposable income using simple time-series estimates for both the dependent and independent variable, and examining if the linear relationship is characterized by a high correlation coefficient and also meets the relevant test of significance, e.g. the 't' test. Similar methods may be used to calculate the value of j. These estimation methods, it will be noted, already assume that a linear model correctly identifies the relationship between the various variables, and, by implication, that the values of the coefficients remain stable throughout the period of time under review. It is claimed by Hansen et al. (cf. op. cit., pp. 46–7) that the use of average values for the coefficients can be defended on the grounds, firstly, that the values chosen are only needed to indicate orders of magnitude, and, secondly, that variations in the value of coefficients, particularly tax rates, are not sufficient to produce a marked change in the value of the multiplier. Using the simple model in equation X.1 and with $b = \frac{3}{4}$, $j = \frac{1}{12}$, and $t_y = \frac{1}{10}$, the value of k, the multiplier, is 2·50. A 100 per cent increase in the average tax rate, making $t_y = \frac{1}{5}$, gives a value of 2·14 for k. Hansen's justification seems reasonable, especially as the variations in tax rates during the period under review were unlikely to be as great as this. However, the finer the 'tuning' necessary in the control of macroeconomic variables by fiscal means, the higher the standard of accuracy required in the estimation of the values of the coefficients.

---

(10) For a similar conclusion in relation to an examination of developing countries, see Morss and Peacock, op. cit.

IV. THE DEVISING OF FISCAL CONTROLS

Consider very briefly the kind of system of public finance which the above analysis suggests is necessary to achieve economic stability in both the short and long run. It requires a satisfactory system of social accounts, a machinery for making economic projections which can indicate with a fair degree of accuracy what the effects of any tax or expenditure change are likely to be over the relevant time period. To carry out any particular line of action through fiscal policy then suggests a further check list of jobs to be done (11):

(a) It must be agreed that the economic model in use is the 'correct' one and will be accepted as such by those responsible for policy. This is a much taller order than it seems. Politicians in power may genuinely believe that they know better than the economists, pointing to the diversity of opinions in the economics profession. The less scrupulous of them may exploit these differences for sectional aims, for the policy measures designed to meet one particular set of political objectives may impose, or appear to impose, costs on those who elect them. Thus, in principle, increasing personal taxes on lower-income groups may be an admirable anti-inflationary device, but does not necessarily appeal to those who have to pay the taxes. Politicians maximize their political life by close attention to the complaints of their constituents.

(b) It must be known in advance what other agencies of economic policy will do, such as the monetary authorities, and, where appropriate, price and wage controlling bodies. This is clear right from the start of our analysis in Chapter II. This points to close co-ordination of the actions of all these bodies, once it is known what the 'shape' of the objective function is likely to be. The chequered history of the growth of co-ordination of economic policy, coupled with the rise of fiscal policy, at least provides some indication that public officials and even economists may be human (12). The growing acceptance of

(11) For more detailed attention to this aspect of fiscal policy, see Alan T. Peacock, 'Fiscal Means and Political Ends', in *Essays in Honour of Lionel Robbins*, forthcoming.
(12) For fascinating accounts of the evolution of fiscal policy in recent years in the US and UK, see Herbert Stein, *The Fiscal Revolution in America*, Chicago, 1969 and Samuel Brittain, *Steering the Economy, The Role of the Treasury*, London, 1969.

'new economics' has naturally encountered strong resistance from public officials whose skills were at least partially rendered obsolescent and who were unwilling or unable to grasp the subtleties of economic analysis. Again, however much economists in government accept in principle the general type of analysis which we have introduced in this volume, it is understandable if their particular special interests and expertise, e.g. as a monetary economist in a Central Bank or as a fiscal economist in a Ministry of Finance, leads them to dramatize the use of the particular instrument of policy for which they are primarily responsible. At least part of the explanation of the controversy over the use of the overall budget balance as an indicator of the stabilization properties of the budget referred to in the previous section arises from the different concerns and responsibilities of the OECD on the one hand and the IMF on the other, the latter emphasizing much more the effects of the budget on the economy which are manifested in changes in liquidity.

(c) Even if complete identity of outlook can be achieved so that economic advisers would go to the stake in support of particular policy measures, it takes time to perfect the tax and expenditure instruments which are necessary to carry them into effect. Even if the perfect administrative measure can be found, its use may be constrained by the constituent elements in the 'objective function', or, in plainer language, the electorate and their representatives may approve of stabilization but may not like the way it is proposed to carry it out. For example, stabilization policy suggests that the central government should exercise a close control over the spending and taxing of 'lower' layers of government, but to one of the authors the exercise of such control conflicts with his desire to see more devolution of governmental power.

Against this background, it may be more readily understandable to the reader why important innovations in fiscal control have had to be introduced, as it were, through the back door and often at a time of national emergency.

One of the most striking examples of this is to be found in the development of Swedish fiscal policy in the 1930s (13). It is a com-

---

(13) For an interesting account of the role of economists in the development of Swedish fiscal policy, see Erik Lundberg, *Business Cycles and Economic Policy*, translated by J. Potter, London, 1957, Chapter V.

plicated story, but, briefly put, budgetary conventions accepted by Parliament demanded that all current expenditure by the government, and 'non-profitable' capital investments should be covered by tax receipts or by profits from public enterprise. After protracted discussion, it was agreed to support the economists' demand that annual balance was too strict a requirement, given the need during the depression conditions in the 1930s to use fiscal action to increase incomes and employment. At the same time, the budget was supposed to balance over the business cycle. A fictional 'Equalization Fund' was set up. The final annual balance of the current budget was not transferred as a receipt (+ for a surplus or − for a deficit) to the capital account, but 'paid into' the Equalization Fund. Thus a compromise between traditional practice and 'new' economic thinking was reached.

The general acceptance of the principle of 'multi-annual' balance has been a mixed blessing in Sweden. In the course of the last two decades it has become increasingly realized in countries inclined to use fiscal measures for stabilization purposes that it is overall budget balance and not merely the current balance which is relevant to policy, as illustrated in Table X.2 of this chapter. Swedish economists have been increasingly critical of emphasis on the 'multi-annual' current balance rule (14) and have accepted the standard reasoning that in formulating fiscal policy, the operating surplus is irrelevant.

Despite official acceptance of the necessity for concentrating attention on total budgetary balance, it is the current budget balance which dominated a good deal of the discussion in the Swedish Parliament and press in the post-war era when surpluses began to accumulate in the fund. A surplus in the Equalization Fund has been taken to mean a case either for more current or capital spending or for a reduction in tax rates and the increase in revenue from state enterprises has gained increasing acceptance for state investment and loans financed from borrowing. It became apparent that the strict following of the 1930s rule of current balance, which would still be

---

(14) See Gösta Rehn, 'Pa vag mot en rationell finanspolitik', *Ide och Handling: Till Ernst Wigfors po 80 årstagen*, Stockholm, 1960, appearing significantly enough in a *Festschrift* for the renowned Finance Minister of the 1930s and 1940s, who introduced the Budgetary Reform of 1937. See also the same author's 'The National Budget and Economic Policy', *Scandinaviska Banken Quarterly Review*, No. 2. 1962, pp. 8–9.

fulfilled if these policies were adopted, conflicted paradoxically enough with a policy of stabilization, that is to say, with the policy which the original budgetary reform was meant to promote!

Looking a little nearer home, it is worth recalling that two major instruments of stabilization policy were introduced without extensive political resistance during the Second World War. As our analysis shows, stabilizing effectiveness, subject to qualifications already discussed in Chapters V and VII, can be improved if tax yields are a function of either income or expenditure and have wide coverage, and the more lags in collections are reduced. Before the Second World War, the British income tax system had a relatively narrow coverage compared with the present day, and the main taxes on expenditure, such as those on tobacco and beer, were not *ad valorem* but specific taxes. The introduction of the Pay-As-You-Earn system of income taxation, and the *ad valorem* purchase tax did much to contribute to the relative success of wartime anti-inflation policy (15). The counterpart to the Swedish economists' preoccupation with the 'inevitability' of the business cycle, which led to multi-annual budgeting, is found in Keynes's famous Post-War Credits scheme. The income tax system was used to introduce compulsory lending by tax-payers to the government, it being assumed that post-war depression would offer the occasion for the government to liquidate its debt to tax-payers just at the time when a boost was necessary to aggregate demand. In the event, the post-war depression never came, and in 1968 over £200 mn. in post-war credits still remained to be paid! Despite the discrediting of compulsory lending it is not certain that we have heard the last of this device, for, given suitable safeguards to lenders, it could be quite a powerful fiscal control (16).

V. CODA

As this book was being written, both authors were involved in a

(15) Cf. R. S. Sayers, *Financial Policy 1939–45*, HMSO, 1956, pp. 99–111 and 126–31.
(16) One of the authors suggested a modernized version of compulsory lending in *The Times*, March 16 and 17, 1968. For a full discussion of compulsory lending schemes in relation to a range of policy objectives, see, A. R. Prest, 'Compulsory Lending Schemes', *Staff Papers*, International Monetary Fund, Vol. XVI, No. 1, 1969.

practical study of methods of creating employment by fiscal means in developing countries with rapid rates of population growth. This has entailed visiting a wide variety of countries with differing emphasis on and commitment to fiscal policy. In one country visited, one government organization did not care to use the national accounts officially submitted to international bodies, such as the UN and IBRD, which, incidentally, were prepared in the Central Bank. Although there was an official planning committee on which all the major economic ministries and the Central Bank was represented there was no document published by it which could be taken to embody a set of economic planning objectives. Whereas detailed study had been made of the effects of the tax system on stability and growth, there was no co-ordination of government expenditure proposals. Different ministries, including the Ministry of Finance, had 'rival' models of the operation of the economy of varying sophistication, which were not necessarily made available to one another. (As one official says, things are so secret in one ministry that when the daily papers arrive, they are believed to be stamped as confidential!) The country concerned had had a decade of a fast rate of growth and relatively stable prices and foreign exchange rate. But over the same period, unemployment had become something of a problem and there had been a definite increase in income inequality.

To the sceptic, this confused picture suggests that even if some commonly accepted objectives were not attained, the economy in question had achieved much, not despite, but because of a political situation which *prevented* policy co-ordination. The enthusiast for economic planning can always answer that one cannot generalize from a sample of one country, and that it is at least conceivable that even in this one instance better articulation of objectives and better policy co-ordination would have produced as good if not better results.

One might resolve this kind of dispute by some kind of cost–benefit study of fiscal planning methods, but this task we must pass over to others. Nevertheless, in taking leave of the reader, we must repeat the warning that whatever technical equipment he may be stimulated to acquire by reading this work, he must not be led to believe that enthusiasm for analysis is necessarily contagious and will take ready hold over those placed in the position of implementing fiscal policy.

Appendix A

SUGGESTIONS FOR ADDITIONAL READING

The following references indicate possible further reading and sources not otherwise indicated in the text.

CHAPTER II

Bailey, M. J. *National Income and the Price Level*, McGraw-Hill, Maidenhead, 1962.

Cary Brown, E. 'The Static Theory of Automatic Fiscal Stabilization', *Journal of Political Economy*, October 1955.

Christ, C. F. 'A Simple Macro-economic Model with a Government Budget Constraint', *Journal of Political Economy*, Jan./Feb. 1968.

Evans, M. K. 'Reconstruction and Estimation of the Balanced Budget Multiplier', *Review of Economics and Statistics*, Feb. 1969.

Forte, Francesco and Hochman, Harold M. 'Monetary and Fiscal Policy: Ambiguities in Definitions', in *Finanz- und Geld-Politik im Umbruch* (eds. Haller and Recktenwald), v. Hase and Koehler, Mainz, 1969.

Hagger, A. 'Multiplier Theory and Fiscal Policy', *Review of Economic Studies*, June 1957.

Haller, H. *Finanzpolitik: Grundlagen und Hauptprobleme*, 4th edition, J. C. B. Mohr (Paul Siebeck), Tübingen, 1968.

Park, R. E. 'Redistributional Aspects of the Balanced Budget Multiplier: A Comment on the Musgrave, Baumol–Preston and Hansen Contributions', *Review of Economics and Statistics*, Vol. XLIX, 1967.

Salant, W. 'Taxes, Income Determination, and the Balanced Budget Multiplier', *Review of Economics and Statistics*, May 1957.

CHAPTER III

Hauser, G. and Burrows, P. *The Economics of Unemployment Insurance*, Allen & Unwin, London, 1969, Ch. 4.

Holzman, F. D. and Zellner, A. 'The Foreign-Trade and Balanced Budget Multipliers', *American Economic Review*, Vol. XLVIII, March 1958.

Shaw, G. K. 'European Economic Integration and Stabilization Policy', in Carl S. Shoup (ed.), *Fiscal Harmonization in Common Markets*, Vol. II, Columbia University Press, 1967.

Thirlwall, A. P. 'Unemployment Compensation as an Automatic Stabilizer', in *Bulletin of the Oxford University Institute of Economics and Statistics*, Feb. 1969.

CHAPTER IV

Engerman, S. 'Regional Aspects of Stabilization Policy', in *Essays in Fiscal Federalism* (ed. R. A. Musgrave), Brookings Institution, Washington 1965.

Peacock, A. T. and Stewart, I. G. 'Fiscal Policy and the Composition of Government Purchases', *Public Finance*, No. 2, 1958.

CHAPTER V

Brooman, F. S. *Macro-economics*, Allen & Unwin, London, 1970, pp. 196–200.

Morag, A. *On Taxes and Inflation*, New York, 1965, esp. Ch. 3.

Williamson, J. 'The Price-Price Spiral', *Yorkshire Bulletin*, May 1967.

CHAPTER VI

Cornwall, J. 'The Structure of Fiscal Policy Models', *Quarterly Journal of Economics*, Vol. LXXIX, 1965.

Hall, Challis A., Jr. *Fiscal Policy for Stable Growth*, Holt, Rinehart & Winston, London, 1960.

Nelson, R. N. 'The Low-Level Equilibrium Population Trap', *American Economic Review*, Dec. 1956.

Peacock, A. T. 'The Public Sector and Economic Growth', *Scottish Journal of Political Economy*, Feb. 1961.
Phelps, Edmund S. *Fiscal Neutrality toward Economic Growth*, McGraw-Hill, Maidenhead, 1965.

CHAPTER VII

Baumol, W. J. 'Pitfalls in Contracyclical Policies: Some Tools and Results', *Review of Economics and Statistics*, Feb. 1961.
Brown, E. C., Solow, R. M., Ando, A. and Karaken, J. 'Lags in Fiscal and Monetary Policy', in *Stabilization Policies, Commission on Money and Credit*, Prentice-Hall, London, 1963.
Friedman, Milton. 'A Monetary and Fiscal Framework for Economic Stability', *American Economic Review*, June 1948.
Rey, Mario. *Saggio Sulla Teoria Della Flessibilità Automatica Fiscale*, Milan, 1968. (This volume contains an excellent bibliography on dynamic aspects of fiscal policy.)
Richter, R. and Selten, R. 'Dynamische Theorie der Built-in Flexibility', *Zeitschrift für die gesamte Staatswissenschaft*, 1963.

CHAPTER VIII

Culbertson, J. M. *Macro-economic Theory and Stabilization Policy*, McGraw-Hill, 1968, Part V.
Helliwell, J. F. 'Monetary and Fiscal Policies for an Open Economy', *Oxford Economic Papers*, March 1969.
Ott, D. J. and Ott, A. F. 'Monetary and Fiscal Policy: Goals and Choice of Instruments', *Quarterly Journal of Economics*, May 1968.
Smith, W. L. 'Monetary–Fiscal Policy and Economic Growth', *Quarterly Journal of Economics*, Feb. 1957.

CHAPTER IX

Fleming, J. Marcus. 'Targets and Instruments', *International Monetary Fund Staff Papers*, Nov. 1968.
Fromm, G. and Taubman, P. *Policy Simulations with an Econometric Model*, Brookings Institution, Washington, 1968, Ch. 5.

Hansen, Bent. *Lectures in Economic Theory: Part II The Theory of Economic Policy and Planning*, Studentlitteratur, Lund, Sweden, 1967.

Theil, H. 'Linear Decision Rules for Macro-Dynamic Policy', in *Quantitative Planning of Economic Policy*, (ed. B. Hickman), Brookings Institution, Washington, 1965.

Tinbergen, J. *Central Planning*, Yale Series in Comparative Economics, 1965.

CHAPTER X

Auld, D. A. L. 'A Measure of Australian Fiscal Policy Performance, 1948–9 to 1963–4', *Economic Record*, Sept. 1967.

Auld, D. A. L. 'An Application of Econometrics to Evaluate Fiscal Tax Policy', *Economic Record*, June 1969.

Auld, D. A. L. 'Fiscal Policy Performance in Canada 1957–67', *Public Finance*, No. 3, 1969.

Balopoulos, E. T. *Fiscal Policy Models of the British Economy*, North-Holland Publishing Company, 1967.

Clark, C. and Stuve, G. (Editors). *Income Redistribution and the Statistical Foundations of Economic Policy*, Income and Wealth Series X. Bowes & Bowes, London, 1964. Articles by Bruno, Ohkawa, Mayer and van den Beld.

Lewis, Wilfred, Jr. (Editor). *Budget Concepts for Economic Analysis*, Brookings Institution, Washington, 1968; especially articles by Galper and Gramlick.

Peacock, A. T. (Editor). *Quantitative Analysis in Public Finance*, Praeger, 1969. Articles by Krupp, Balopoulos, Morss and Peacock.

Sandee, J. and van de Pas, J. H. 'The Effect of Fluctuations in Public Expenditure and Taxation on Economic Growth', in *Public Economics* (ed. J. Margolis and H. Guitton), Macmillan, for International Economic Association, 1969.

Smyth, D. J. 'The Measurement of Fiscal Performance', *Economic Record*, December 1968.

Appendix B

THE MAIN SYMBOLS USED

B	Balance of payments
B^K	Capital account of balance of payments
C	Consumption
C_c	Consumption per capita
C^m	Consumption in monetary units
D	Budget deficit/surplus $= T - G$.
E	Function
G	Government expenditures
G_d	Government defence expenditures
G^m	Government expenditures in monetary units
H	Autonomous element in government expenditure
I	Investment
I^m	Investment in monetary units
I_x	Investment *ex ante*
K	Capital stock
K_c	Capital per capita
K^m	Capital stock in monetary units
L	Total demand for money
L^t	Transactions demand for money
L^s	Speculative demand for money
M	Imports
MS	Money stock
N	Units of employment or labour input
N^a	Average product of labour
NW	Total wages
O	Profits
P	Price or price index
P^c	Price level of consumption goods
P^i	Price level of investment goods

204

P^K	Price level of capital goods
PQ	Total revenue = Money national income
Q	National output
R	Transfer payments
S	Savings
S_c	Savings per capita
T	Total tax yield
T_i	Indirect taxes
T_y	Income taxes
U	Unemployment
V	Input
V_N	Labour input
V^K	Capital input
W	Total wage
X	Exports
Y	Gross national product/income
Y^c	Capacity income
Y_c	Income per capita
Y^d	Disposable income
Y^F	Full employment income
Y^m	Money national income
Y_f^m	Money national income at factor cost
Y^g	Actual growth of income
Y^r	Required or equilibrium growth of income
Y^*	Target growth of income
Z	Sum of all autonomous expenditures

CONSTANTS, EXOGENOUSLY DETERMINED PARAMETERS, ETC.

Δ	Increase
Σ	Sum of
Π	Mathematical function
θ	Shift parameter
Φ	Shift parameter
α	Autonomous consumption—i.e. consumption at zero income
β	Autonomous investment—i.e. investment at zero interest and/or zero income
γ	Speculative demand for money at zero interest rate

∂ Partial derivative
ψ Exogenous growth rate of population
λ Lagrange multiplier
η Taxes at zero income—e.g. lump sum taxes
π Societies objective function
σ Output–capital ratio
μ Stabilization or fiscal coefficient
Ω Accelerator coefficient
ϕ Incremental capital output ratio
$\left.\begin{array}{l}\varepsilon \\ \zeta\end{array}\right\}$ Non-defined constants
ρ Investment ratio

COEFFICIENTS, FUNCTIONAL RELATIONSHIPS, RATIOS, ETC.

b Marginal propensity to consume
c Interest-elasticity coefficient of the speculative demand for money
e Natural log
f Function of
g Ratio of government expenditures to national income
h Marginal propensity of government expenditure
i Rate of interest
j Marginal propensity to import
k Multiplier
k_a 'Domestic' multiplier of country A—i.e. excludes the element of foreign repercussion
l Commodity l
m Commodity m
n Time
p Percentage of government expenditures of an investment nature
q Interest–investment coefficient
r Capital–labour ratio $= K/N$
s Savings ratio $= S/Y$
s' Savings ratio after tax
t_y Rate of income tax
t_i Indirect tax rate

u Utility index
v Transactions demand for money coefficient
w Wage rate
x
y }   Policy objectives
z

Notes

(1) Time derivative $\dfrac{d(\ \ )}{dn}$ indicated by $(\ \dot{}\ )$. Thus $\dfrac{dY}{dn} = \dot{Y}$

(2) The placing of a bar over a symbol implies that it is being held constant or is autonomously determined. Thus, for example, $\bar{G}$ indicates a constant level of government expenditure.

(3) Subscripts a, b, and n:
 Any of the symbols used above may be modified by the use of three commonly employed subscripts. The first two, a and b, define an economic variable, magnitude or coefficient exclusively with respect to two countries A and B. Thus, for example,
 Y_a^d refers to disposable income in country A,
 Y_b^d to disposable income in country B.
 The subscript n defines the time period concerned. Thus whilst
 Y_n^c denotes capacity income at time period n,
 Y_{n-2}^c indicates the same concept two periods (years) ago.

(4) Superscripts A and B:
 In a like manner the above symbols may be modified by the use of two commonly adopted superscripts A and B. These define a variable specifically with respect to an individual or industry. Hence
 V^A = the input of industry A,
 u^A = the utility of individual A
 and so forth.

NAME INDEX

Ackley, Gardner, 15n, 28n
Allen, R. G. D., 13n
Ames, Edward, 66n
Ando, A., 202
Archibald, G. C., 25n, 36n
Auld, D. A. L., 203

Bailey, M. J., 200
Balopoulos, E. T., 203
Baumol, W. J., 120n, 202
Biehl, Dieter, 190n
Bombach, Gottfried, 96n, 118n, 126n
Brittain, Samuel, 195n
Bronfenbrenner, Martin, 18n
Brooman, N. S., 201
Brown, E. C., 89n, 200, 202
Burrows, P., 201

Christ, C. F., 200
Clark, C., 203
Cooper, R. N., 138
Cornwall, J., 97n, 201
Culbertson, J. M., 202

Dernberg, T. E., 19n
Domar, E. D., 13, 19, 96, 97, 98, 99n,
    100, 101, 102, 110, 126, 160
Dosser, D. G. M., 110n

Engerman, S., 201
Evans, M. K., 200

Fleming, J. Marcus, 202
Forte, Francesco, 200
Friedman, Milton, 202
Fromm, Gary, 192n, 202

Gelting, J., 32, 35

Haavelmo, T., 32, 35

Hagger, A., 200
Hahn, F. H., 20n
Hall, Challis A., Jnr, 201
Haller, H., 200
Hansen, A. H., 41, 42, 52, 54
Hansen, Bent, 13n, 23n, 141, 142, 158,
    190, 191n, 193, 194
Harrod, R. F., 13, 19, 96, 97, 98n, 100,
    101, 110, 126, 160
Hauser, G., 201
Helliwell, J. F., 202
Hicks, J. R., 13, 41, 42, 52, 54, 63,
    63n, 120n
Hochman, Harold M., 200
Holzman, F. D., 18n, 201

Johansen, L., 13n
Johnson, H. G., 105n

Kaldor, N., 13
Kalecki, M., 13
Karaken, J., 202
Keynes, J. M., 17, 29, 39, 40, 198
Kilpatrick, Robert W., 10, 50n

Lefeber, Louis, 175n
Leontieff, W., 71
Lewis, Wilfred, Jnr, 203
Lipsey, R. G., 25n, 36n
Lundberg, Erik, 196n

Matthews, R. C. O., 20n
Maurice, Rita, 177n
McDougall, D. M., 19n
Miller, M. H., 118n
Morag, A., 201
Morss, Elliott, 190n, 194n
Mundell, R. A., 142n, 143, 146, 147
Musgrave, Peggy, 190n, 191n
Musgrave, R. A., 13n, 89n, 97n, 118n,
    182, 190n, 191n, 201

o   209

SUBJECT INDEX

Accelerator, 98n, 119
  See also Multiplier–Accelerator
Accelerator Coefficient
  Uncertainty of, 61
Ad Valorem Tax, 87, 91, 198
Aggregate Supply, *ex ante*, 90
Aggregate Supply Function, 18, 165
Automatic Monetary Stability, 43, 45
Automatic Stabilization, 35, 36, 116,
  132n
  In a Dynamic Setting, 96n, 125f
Automatic Stabilizers, 14, 35, 36, 117,
  118, 133, 139n
  Destabilizing Consequences of, 96,
  118n, 125n
  Versus Discretionary Policy, 21, 117,
  124, 133

Balance of Payments Deficit
  Constraint of, 27, 82
Balance of Trade Effect
  Of a Price Change, 93
Balanced Budget
  Multiplier Effects of, 14, 184
Balanced Budget Change, 33, 34, 43,
  100, 137, 172
Balanced Budget Multiplier, 32f, 137,
  147, 148
Balanced Budget Multiplier Theorem,
  47, 63
Balanced Budget Theorem, 32
Budget Accounts
  And Economic Stability, 182
  And Growth Policy, 184f
  Stabilization Budget Versus 'Tradi-
  tional', 182, 185
Budget Accounts for Economic Stabi-
  lity
  Classification of, 183
Budget Surplus
  As Index of Fiscal Policy, 143, 147

Built-In Flexibility, 118, 118n, 125f,
  132, 189n
  And Economic Growth, 96
  Distinguished from Automatic
  Stabilization, 118n, 132n
Built-In Stability, 21
  Of Monetary Sector, 39–45

Cobb–Douglas Production Function,
  19, 101–104, 110, 170n
Common Markets
  Formation of, 49
  Joining of, 30
Comparative Statics, 20
  Limitations of, 62
Comparative Static Methodology, 115
Constant Returns to Scale, 102
Consumption Function, 28, 30f, 93f,
  118f
Consumption Multiplier, 30
Consumption Tax
  Versus Income Tax re Output,
  Employment & Prices, 88f
Cost Benefit Analysis, 63, 185, 199
Cost Push Inflation, 90
Credit Multiplier, 138

Debt Finance, 43, 44
Developing Countries
  And Actual Planning Models, 175
  And Employment Creation, 164f
  And Input–Output Tables, 168
  And Keynesian Policies, 164f
  And Statistical Services, 187, 188
  And Surplus Labour, 113, 114
Diminishing Returns, 29, 39, 102, 104

Economic Union
  And Destabilizing Income Movements, 50

211

For Product Safety Concerns and Information please contact our EU
representative GPSR@taylorandfrancis.com
Taylor & Francis Verlag GmbH, Kaufingerstraße 24, 80331 München, Germany

www.ingramcontent.com/pod-product-compliance
Ingram Content Group UK Ltd.
Pitfield, Milton Keynes, MK11 3LW, UK
UKHW021824240425
457818UK00006B/62